200 healthy chinese recipes

D1216282

hamlyn | **all colour cookbook**

200 healthy chinese recipes

Sunil Vijayakar

An Hachette UK company
www.hachette.co.uk

First published in Great Britain in 2013 by Hamlyn,
a division of Octopus Publishing Group Ltd
Endeavour House, 189 Shaftesbury Avenue
London WC2H 8JY
www.octopusbooks.co.uk

ISBN: 978 0 60062 682 4

A CIP catalogue record for this book is available from the
British Library

Printed and bound in China

1 2 3 4 5 6 7 8 9 10

Both metric and imperial measurements have been given
in all recipes. Use one set of measurements only, and not
a mixture of both.

Standard level spoon measurements are used in all recipes.
1 tablespoon = one 15 ml spoon
1 teaspoon = one 5 ml spoon

Ovens should be preheated to the specified temperature –
if using a fan-assisted oven, follow the manufacturer's
instructions for adjusting the time and the temperature.

Fresh herbs should be used unless otherwise stated.
Medium eggs should be used unless otherwise stated.

The Department of Health advises that eggs should not
be consumed raw. This book contains some dishes made
with raw or lightly cooked eggs. It is prudent for vulnerable
people such as pregnant and nursing mothers, invalids,
the elderly, babies and young children to avoid uncooked
or lightly cooked dishes made with eggs. Once prepared,
these dishes should be kept refrigerated and used promptly.

This book includes dishes made with nuts and nut
derivatives. It is advisable for those with known allergic
reactions to nuts and nut derivatives and those who may
be potentially vulnerable to these allergies to avoid dishes
made with nuts and nut oils. It is also prudent to check the
labels of pre-prepared ingredients for the possible inclusion
of nut derivatives.

contents

introduction

introduction

In China, food and its preparation have been developed so highly that it has reached the status of an art form. Both rich and poor, Chinese people consider that delicious and nutritious food is a basic necessity of life.

The great ancient Chinese philosopher Confucius emphasized the artistic and social aspects of cooking and eating, and in China it is considered poor etiquette to invite friends to your home without providing something appropriate to eat. In fact, Chinese people simply don't gather together without there being food involved. The ancient Chinese philosophy of Taoism, on the other hand, encouraged research into the nourishment provided by food and cooking. Rather than concentrating on taste and appearance, Taoists were more interested in the health-giving and life-enhancing properties of food. Centuries on, the Chinese have discovered the health-promoting properties of all sorts of ingredients. They have taught the world that the nutritional value of vegetables is destroyed by overcooking (particularly boiling), and have discovered and demonstrated that ingredients with a great flavour also have medicinal value.

Home-cooked Chinese food is extremely healthy, due to the use of very small quantities of polyunsaturated oils and the exclusion of dairy products. Although many Chinese restaurants in the West prepare their menu using highly

saturated fats, authentic Chinese food is arguably the healthiest on the planet. All the recipes in this book involve a minimal amount of oil, and most use low-calorie cooking spray.

The Chinese approach to cooking is one of the greatest there has ever been, and many factors have influenced its development from ancient times to the present day. Confucius once said, 'Eating is the utmost important thing in life', and Chinese cuisine is considered a highly sophisticated art, requiring much time and consideration.

cooking styles in China: Beijing, Szechuan, Hunan and Cantonese, though still many provincial variations and ethnic minority specialities.

Beijing

Beijing cuisine is also known as Mandarin cuisine. Many of the foods in this region are wheat-based (as opposed to rice-based), so Beijing cuisine consists of a variety of dumplings, baked and steamed breads and various types of noodle. Mandarin-style meals usually include vegetable dishes, soups, tofu (soya bean curd) and fish. The food is mild in taste, and vinegar and garlic are common ingredients. Dishes are frequently stewed or braised, while dumplings are filled with a meat or vegetable mixture and steamed.

A meal in Chinese culture is typically seen as consisting of two basic components: a main food, which is a source of carbohydrate or starch, typically rice (predominant in southern parts of China) or noodles (predominant in northern parts of China); and accompanying dishes of vegetables, seafood, fish, meat and poultry.

Chinese regional cooking styles

As China is a huge country geographically, it is diverse in climate, ethnicity and subcultures. Not surprisingly, therefore, there are many distinctive styles of cuisine. Historically there were eight great culinary traditions (Anhui, Guandong, Fujian, Hunan, Jiangsu, Shandong, Szechuan and Zhejian). Today there are four main regional

Szechuan

Food from the Szechuan (or 'Four Rivers') basin is characteristic of the south-western region of China. Featuring a liberal use of garlic, ginger, spring onion and chilli, Szechuan food is distinguished by its hot, peppery flavours. It is the spiciest style of Chinese cooking and certainly very tasty.

Hunan

The traditional cuisine of Hunan Province is richer than that of Szechuan and may be either spicy or sweet and sour. Chicken, pork, fish and shellfish are all popular ingredients cooked in this manner.

Cantonese

From Canton or Guangdong Province in the south-eastern region of China (which includes Hong Kong), Cantonese cuisine is the mildest and most widely consumed type of Chinese food in the world. Cantonese food tends to be more colourful and less spicy than the other regional styles of cooking and is usually stir-fried, which preserves both the texture and flavour of ingredients. Dim sum or 'tea lunch', usually consisting of tasty little dumplings and pastries stuffed with meats and vegetables, is served at many Cantonese restaurants during the lunch hour. Freshness is supreme to the Cantonese, and sauces are kept mild and subtle so as not to overpower the fresh taste of the ingredients.

Healthy principles

The Chinese way of looking at health lies in one of the fundamental principles of its traditional philosophy, that food and medicine share the same roots. The firm belief that food has healing powers and therapeutic effects has led to the cultivation of many different edible plants and herbs in China, and as the benefits of disease prevention and health preservation that they offer have been recognized, so they have become standard ingredients in Chinese home-cooked dishes. At the same time, there has been a pursuit of refinement in Chinese cooking. The quantities of different ingredients and their combination are essential considerations. Whether making main dishes or soups, foods are combined according to their relative nutritional content to achieve the goal of an overall balance in nutritional intake. And it is recommended to eat only until the stomach is about 70–80% full, a practice that has been passed down through the generations as a secret to long life.

Equipment

The beauty of cooking Chinese food in your home is that you don't need much specialist equipment at all. The two main pieces of equipment are the wok and the bamboo steamer.

Wok

Key to Chinese cooking, the wok is the heart of the Chinese kitchen. There is almost no limit to the number of delicious dishes that can come out of this unassuming piece of equipment on the hob. It is one of the most useful and versatile pans available, as it can be used for stir-frying, blanching and steaming foods as well as deep-frying. Its shape, with deep sides and a rounded bottom, allows for fuel-efficient, quick and even heating and cooking. This quick-cooking method also preserves the vitamins in the vegetables. Traditional-style woks need to be seasoned and tempered before using, but the recipes in this book feature a good-quality nonstick wok that doesn't need to be prepared before use and also requires the barest minimum of

oil for cooking, thus making your dishes even healthier. You can use a large, deep nonstick frying pan in place of a wok if you need to.

Steamer

Steaming is essential to much of Chinese cooking. The best option is to buy one or more inexpensive bamboo steamers, which come in a wide range of sizes, the 25 cm (10 inch) size being the most practical for the home cook. The food is placed in the steamer and that in turn is placed above boiling water in a wok or large saucepan. A tight-fitting bamboo lid prevents the steam from escaping.

To make the best use of your bamboo steamer, follow these simple instructions:

1 Fill the wok or pan roughly one-third with water. It is very important that you use the right amount of water – too little and the water can boil off and scald the wok; too much and it will boil up on to the food.

2 Bring the water to the boil over a medium heat – wait until you see a rolling boil.

3 Carefully arrange your food inside the bamboo steamer – you can stack several bamboo steamer baskets on top of one another to cook different foods at the same time. Place food that cooks quickly in the top basket and food that takes a little longer in the bottom basket. Place the lid on the top basket.

4 Carefully place the steamer in your wok or pan. Allow the water to boil rapidly and circulate inside the steamer, evenly cooking the food. Cooking times will vary depending on the food you are cooking.

5 Clean your bamboo steamers by washing them by hand with gentle washing-up liquid and water. Don't soak them in the sink or put them in the dishwasher, as this can ruin the bamboo. Allow the steamers to air-dry completely before putting them away.

STEAMING TIPS

* Place a layer of cabbage or lettuce underneath the food in the steamer to prevent the food from sticking to the steamer, or line it with nonstick baking paper. This is very helpful when steaming sticky foods like dumplings or wontons.

* To avoid steam burns, always lift the lid of the steamer away from your body. Wrist burns can occur if steam or hot water are expelled as you lift the lid, so use caution. Use pot-holders to set up and remove steamers.

Ingredients

All the various Chinese ingredients you need are widely available these days in most supermarkets and grocery stores. However, some specialized foods and ingredients may only be found in Chinese and Asian supermarkets or from online suppliers.

Bamboo shoots

Fresh bamboo shoots have a distinctive taste, but are quite difficult to obtain. Canned sliced bamboo shoots are widely available and have a sweet flavour and crunchy texture.

Bitter melon

This unusual-looking vegetable has a bumpy green skin and a slightly bitter taste, and is valued for its medicinal qualities.

Fermented black beans

Also known as salted beans or preserved beans, these small black soya beans have a distinctive salty taste and rich aroma, and are used as a seasoning, usually with ginger, garlic and chilli. You can buy them in jars or cans.

Chilli bean paste

This is made from a mixture of ground chillies, salt, garlic and oil that has been fermented to form a rich paste, and is used as a seasoning in Chinese dishes.

Chilli sauce

Made from chillies, vinegar, sugar and salt, this bright red sauce is sometimes used in Chinese cooking but mainly as a dipping sauce or to add heat to any dish.

Chinese sausage (lap chong)

These thin sausages about 15 cm (6 inches) in length are made from cured duck liver, pork liver or pork. They are used to season rice and poultry dishes, and must be cooked before being eaten.

Cinnamon

In Chinese cooking, the cinnamon bark's aromatic flavour is widely used in braised dishes and is one of the ingredients in Chinese five-spice powder.

Dried Chinese mushrooms

Dried Chinese mushrooms need to be rehydrated in hot water before using. They have an intense meaty flavour and the soaking liquid is often used in place of stock in a sauce. The flesh is usually finely chopped and sautéed in Chinese vegetable dishes.

Hoisin sauce

Part of the bean sauce family, this rich, thick and dark sauce is made from soya bean paste, garlic, vinegar, sugar and spices.

Noodles

Egg noodles are made from wheat flour and eggs, and are available fresh and dried. They come in different thicknesses and are usually yellowish in colour. They are used in stir-fries as well as soups.

Rice noodles are made from rice flour, wheat starch and water, and are available fresh and dried.

Bean thread noodles (also known as transparent or cellophane noodles) are made from ground mung beans. They are available dried and are very fine and white in colour. Once soaked, they become soft and translucent.

Oyster sauce

This popular southern Chinese sauce is thick and brown with a rich taste. Made from oysters, soy sauce and spices, it is highly versatile and adds a boost of flavour to many dishes.

Preserved cabbage

Cabbage leaves are pickled in a mixture of salt, vinegar and sugar, and used as a seasoning. Preserved cabbage is available in cans and should always be rinsed before using.

Rice

Long-grain rice is the most popular type of rice in Chinese cooking and there are many different varieties.

Rice vinegar

Used widely in Chinese cooking and made from rice and grains, rice vinegar has a sweet, tart and slightly pungent flavour. Black rice vinegar is dark in colour and is used in braised dishes and sauces.

Sesame oil

A highly aromatic oil made from sesame seeds, this is used as a flavouring in very small quantities in many Chinese dishes.

Shaoxing rice wine

This amber-coloured Chinese matured rice wine is widely used in Chinese cooking.

A dry pale sherry can be substituted for it in any of the recipes.

Soy sauce

Used in China more than 3,000 years ago, this sauce is made from fermented soya beans, flour and water and is then distilled. There are two main types of soy sauce: dark and light. Light soy is light in colour, full of flavour and widely used in Chinese cooking. It is slightly saltier than dark soy sauce. Dark soy sauce is aged for longer than the light variety and is therefore thicker and darker.

Spring roll wrappers

These paper-thin pastry skins made from flour and water are used for making spring rolls and are about 15 cm (6 inches) square. They can be bought ready-made frozen in packets and need to be thawed before using.

Szechuan or Sichuan peppercorns

These are dried berries from a shrub, and have a sharp, slightly numbing effect on the tongue with a clean lemony spiciness. They are one of the components of Chinese five-spice powder.

Star anise

This star-shaped, aromatic liquorice-flavoured seedpod is widely used in braising, imparting a rich fragrance. It is also an ingredient in Chinese five-spice powder.

Tofu

Also known as doufu or soya bean curd, tofu plays an important part in Chinese cooking. It is highly nutritious, rich in protein and very low in saturated fats. It is easy to digest, inexpensive and very versatile. Made from yellow soya beans, tofu is usually sold in two main forms, firm and silken.

Water chestnuts

Fresh water chestnuts add crunch and texture to many Chinese dishes, but are difficult to obtain. Canned water chestnuts, however, are widely available.

Wonton wrappers

Made from egg and flour, these wrappers are used for dim sum, wontons and dumplings, and are available fresh or frozen. They are sold in packets and are about 7 cm (3 inches) square. If frozen, defrost before using.

Yellow bean sauce

Also known as bean sauce, this thick, spicy fermented sauce is made from yellow beans, flour and salt. It adds spicy–aromatic flavour to dishes and is available in jars in Chinese supermarkets.

Getting started

Don't be hampered by the misconception that Chinese food is difficult to prepare at home. It really doesn't demand any more skill, effort or time than any other type of cooking. As long as you have a few key storecupboard ingredients and a large wok or nonstick frying pan you can cook most dishes in this book. Many of the recipes in this book take less than 20 minutes to cook, and a big plus point is that you can do a lot of the preparation ahead of time, such as chopping the vegetables, which makes it so much quicker and easier when it comes to cooking the dish.

By buying this book, you have decided to take the plunge and start cooking healthy Chinese food. Congratulations! All the recipes in this book have been specially selected as being low in fat. Prepared properly, Chinese food can be beneficial to your whole well-being, as well as being full of flavour.

soups & starters

soy tofu salad with coriander

Serves **4**

Preparation time **10 minutes**,
  plus standing

500 g (1 lb) **firm tofu**, drained

6 **spring onions**, finely
  shredded

10 tablespoons roughly
  chopped **coriander leaves**

1 large **mild red chilli**,
  deseeded and finely sliced

4 tablespoons **light soy sauce**

2 teaspoons **sesame oil**

Cut the tofu into bite-sized cubes and carefully arrange
on a serving plate in a single layer. Sprinkle over the
spring onions, coriander and chilli.

Drizzle over the soy sauce and oil, then leave to stand
at room temperature for 10 minutes before serving.

For steamed chilli-soy tofu, drain 500 g (1 lb) firm
tofu, cut it into cubes and place it on a heatproof plate
that will fit inside a bamboo steamer. Cover and steam
over a wok or large saucepan of boiling water (see
page 14) for 20 minutes, then drain off the excess
water and carefully transfer to a serving plate. Heat
4 tablespoons light soy sauce, 1 tablespoon each
sesame oil and groundnut oil and 2 teaspoons oyster
sauce in a small saucepan until hot. Pour over the
tofu, scatter with 4 thinly sliced spring onions, 1 finely
chopped red chilli and a small handful of finely chopped
coriander leaves and serve.

winter cabbage & ginger soup

Serves **4**
Preparation time **10 minutes**
Cooking time **15 minutes**

1.2 litres (2 pints) boiling hot
   chicken or **vegetable stock**
400 g (13 oz) **Chinese
   cabbage**, roughly chopped
2 tablespoons peeled and
   finely chopped **fresh root
   ginger**
2 **star anise**
2 tablespoons **light soy sauce**
½ teaspoon **sesame oil**
white pepper

Place the stock in a large saucepan and bring to the boil.

Add the cabbage, ginger and star anise to the stock,
return to the boil and cook for 10–12 minutes.

Remove from the heat and stir in the soy sauce and oil,
season with white pepper and ladle into warmed bowls
to serve.

For stir-fried Chinese cabbage with ginger & garlic,

remove and discard the outer leaves from ½ Chinese
cabbage and cut into large pieces. Pound 3 garlic cloves
with a large pinch of salt in a mortar with a pestle until
coarsely ground. Heat a wok or large nonstick frying
pan over a high heat, add 2 tablespoons groundnut oil
and heat until almost smoking. Add the garlic and
1 tablespoon peeled and grated fresh root ginger,
then immediately add the cabbage and stir-fry, moving
the pan contents constantly to prevent the garlic from
burning. Cook until the cabbage is heated through but
still crunchy. Transfer to a warmed serving plate and
season with white pepper before serving.

salmon & spinach dim sum

Makes **28**
Preparation time **30 minutes,**
  plus cooling
Cooking time **20 minutes**

low-calorie cooking spray
1 **carrot,** finely diced
1 tablespoon peeled and finely
  chopped **fresh root ginger**
1 **garlic clove,** crushed
4 **spring onions,** finely
  chopped
½ teaspoon **sesame oil**
100 g (3½ oz) **baby spinach
  leaves,** finely shredded
250 g (8 oz) piece of skinless
  salmon fillet
1 **egg white**
2 tablespoons **cornflour**
28 **fresh wonton wrappers**
4 tablespoons **Shaoxing rice
  wine**
4 tablespoons **light soy sauce**
salt

Spray a nonstick frying pan with cooking spray and heat over a medium heat. Add the carrot, ginger, garlic and spring onions and cook, stirring, for 5 minutes. Stir in the sesame oil and spinach and cook for a few seconds until the spinach has wilted. Increase the heat and cook for 1 minute until any liquid has evaporated. Leave to cool.

Purée the salmon in a food processor. Whisk the egg white with the cornflour in a large bowl, then add the salmon, the vegetable mixture and salt to taste and mix thoroughly.

Spoon 1 teaspoon of the fish mixture in the centre of a wonton wrapper. Dampen the wrapper edges with water and bring up the sides around the filling. Pinch the the top to seal. Repeat with the remaining wrappers and fish mixture. (You can refrigerate, covered with clingfilm, for up to 12 hours before cooking.)

Place without touching in a stacking bamboo steamer lined with nonstick baking paper, cover and steam (see page 14) for 8–10 minutes until cooked through. If you don't have stacking baskets, steam in 2 batches and keep the cooked batch hot over a saucepan of simmering water while cooking the second batch.

Meanwhile, mix the rice wine and soy sauce together in a small bowl and serve with the dim sum.

For sweet chilli dipping sauce, place 1 deseeded and chopped red pepper, 2 halved red chillies, 100 g (3½ oz) caster sugar and 100 ml (3½ fl oz) each of rice vinegar and cold water in a saucepan. Bring to the boil, then simmer for 30 minutes until it turns pinkish. Cool, then process in a blender until smooth. Return to the pan and simmer for 20 minutes until slightly sticky. Cool and serve.

mushroom & ginger wontons

Serves **4**
Preparation time **30 minutes**,
 plus cooling
Cooking time **10–12 minutes**

2 tablespoons **vegetable oil**
1 **garlic clove**, crushed
1 teaspoon peeled and grated
 fresh root ginger
250 g (8 oz) **mixed
 mushrooms**, trimmed and
 finely chopped
1 tablespoon **dark soy sauce**
1 tablespoon chopped
 coriander
16 **fresh wonton wrappers**
salt and **pepper**

Dressing
1 teaspoon **dried chilli flakes**
150 ml (¼ pint) **vegetable
 stock**
1 tablespoon **rice vinegar**
1 tablespoon **light soy sauce**
2 teaspoons **caster sugar**
¼ teaspoon freshly ground
 Szechuan pepper

Heat the oil in a frying pan over a medium heat, add the garlic and ginger and stir-fry for 2–3 minutes. Add the mushrooms and soy sauce and cook, stirring, for 3–4 minutes until golden. Remove from the heat, season to taste with salt and pepper and stir in the coriander. Leave to cool.

Meanwhile, place all the ingredients for the dressing in a saucepan and heat over a low heat, stirring, until hot but not boiling. Keep warm.

Lay a wonton wrapper in the palm of one hand. Place 1 teaspoon of the mushroom mixture in the centre. Dampen the wrapper edges with water, then fold the wrapper in half diagonally and press the edges together to seal and form a parcel. (You can refrigerate, covered with clingfilm, for up to 12 hours before cooking.)

Bring a large saucepan of lightly salted water to a rolling boil, add the wontons and cook for 2–3 minutes until they rise to the surface. Gently drain and transfer to warmed bowls. Strain the dressing over and serve.

For crispy mushroom wontons, heat 5 cm (2 inches) vegetable oil in a wok or deep, heavy-based saucepan until it reaches 180–190°C (350–375°F), or until a cube of bread browns in 30 seconds. Add the wontons, in batches, and deep-fry for 2–3 minutes until crisp and golden. Remove with a slotted spoon and drain on kitchen paper. Serve with Sweet Chilli Dipping Sauce (see page 26).

chicken noodle soup

Serves **4**
Preparation time **10 minutes**,
  plus cooling
Cooking time **40 minutes**

2 **chicken quarters**, about
  750 g (1½ lb) in total
1 **onion**, chopped
4 **garlic cloves**, chopped
3 slices of **fresh root ginger**,
  peeled and bruised
2 litres (3½ pints) **cold water**
125 g (4 oz) **dried fine egg
  noodles**
2 tablespoons **light soy sauce**
1 **red bird's eye chilli**,
  deseeded and sliced
2 **spring onions**, sliced
2 tablespoons **coriander
  leaves**
salt and **pepper**

Place the chicken quarters, onion, garlic, ginger, measurement water and salt and pepper to taste in a saucepan. Bring to the boil, then reduce the heat and simmer gently, uncovered, for 30 minutes, skimming off any scum that rises to the surface.

Remove the chicken, strain the stock and leave to cool. Meanwhile, when cool enough to handle, skin the chicken and shred the flesh.

Cook the noodles in a saucepan of boiling water according to the packet instructions, until just tender. Drain well and divide between 4 warmed bowls.

Heat the reserved stock in a saucepan with the soy sauce. Add the chicken and simmer for 5 minutes.

Spoon the stock and chicken over the noodles and sprinkle over the chilli, spring onion and coriander leaves. Serve immediately.

For aromatic chicken noodle soup, cook the chicken quarters with the other ingredients in the water as above, adding 6 large torn kaffir lime leaves. Remove the chicken and strain the stock, then skin the chicken and shred as above. Heat the stock in a saucepan with 2 tablespoons fish sauce, juice of ½ lime, 2 teaspoons caster sugar and 1 deseeded and sliced red bird's eye chilli. Add the chicken and simmer for 5 minutes. Meanwhile, place 125 g (4 oz) dried rice noodles in a large heatproof bowl, pour over boiling hot water to cover and leave to stand for 5 minutes, or until just tender, then drain. Serve the noodles with the stock and chicken spooned over, garnished with sliced chillies, coriander leaves and shredded kaffir lime leaves.

black tea & star anise eggs

Serves **4**
Preparation time **10 minutes**,
  plus cooling and standing
Cooking time **2¼ hours**

8 eggs
750 ml (1¼ pints) **water**
1 tablespoon **light soy sauce**
1 tablespoon **dark soy sauce**
2 tablespoons **black tea
  leaves**
2 **star anise**
1 **cinnamon stick**
1 tablespoon finely grated
  orange rind
salt
crisp lettuce leaves, to serve

Place the eggs in a large saucepan with 1 teaspoon salt and cover with cold water. Bring to the boil, then reduce the heat and simmer for 12 minutes. Remove from the heat, drain and leave to cool. When cool, tap the eggs with the back of a spoon to crack the shells all over, but don't remove the shells.

Combine the measurement water , soy sauces, ¼ teaspoon salt, tea leaves, star anise, cinnamon stick and orange rind in a large saucepan. Bring to the boil, then reduce the heat, cover and simmer for 2 hours. Remove from the heat, add the eggs and leave to stand for at least 8–12 hours.

Shell the eggs and cut in half, then serve with crisp lettuce leaves.

For Chinese-style open egg omelette, spray a nonstick ovenproof frying pan with low-calorie cooking spray and heat over a high heat. Add 6 sliced spring onions, 2 chopped garlic cloves and 1 finely chopped deseeded red chilli and stir-fry for 1–2 minutes. Add 1 tablespoon each of oyster sauce, light soy sauce and sweet chilli sauce and cook, stirring, for 1–2 minutes. Beat together 6 eggs in a bowl and stir in 4 tablespoons chopped coriander leaves. Season with salt and pepper and pour into the pan. Cook over a medium heat for about10–12 minutes, or until the underside is starting to set. Transfer the pan to a preheated medium-high grill and cook for 4–5 minutes, or until the top is set and golden. Remove from the grill and serve warm or at room temperature.

spinach, mushroom & tofu broth

Serves **4**
Preparation time **20 minutes**,
  plus soaking
Cooking time **10 minutes**

4 **dried Chinese mushrooms**
8 large fresh **shiitake
  mushrooms**
low-calorie cooking spray
2 **garlic cloves**, finely chopped
¼ teaspoon **chilli paste**
1 teaspoon **Shaoxing rice
  wine**
1.2 litres (2 pints) boiling hot
  vegetable stock
1 teaspoon **light soy sauce**
½ teaspoon **golden caster
  sugar**
1 tablespoon **cornflour**, mixed
  to a paste with 2 tablespoons
  cold water
400 g (13 oz) **firm tofu**,
  drained and cut into
  bite-sized cubes
400 g (13 oz) **baby spinach
  leaves**
½ teaspoon **sesame oil**
pepper

Place the dried mushrooms in a heatproof bowl, pour over boiling hot water to cover and leave to soak for 30 minutes until softened. Drain and squeeze out the excess water. Remove and discard the stems, and thinly slice the caps. Trim and then thinly slice the fresh mushrooms.

Spray a nonstick wok or frying pan with cooking spray and heat over a medium-high heat. Add the garlic and chilli paste and stir-fry for a few seconds until aromatic. Add the mushrooms and stir-fry for 2 minutes.

Stir the rice wine into the pan, followed by the stock, soy sauce, sugar and cornflour paste. Season to taste with pepper. Bring to the boil, stirring constantly, then stir in the tofu and spinach. Return to the boil and cook, stirring, for 2–3 minutes until the spinach turns bright green and the mixture has thickened.

Remove the pan from the heat and stir in the sesame oil. Ladle into warmed bowls and serve immediately.

For spinach, tomato & tofu salad, place 100 g (3½ oz) baby spinach leaves in a salad bowl with 400 g (13 oz) halved cherry tomatoes and 400 g (13 oz) firm tofu, drained and cut into bite-sized cubes. Mix together 2 tablespoons each of light soy sauce and sweet chilli sauce, 1 tablespoon sesame oil and 1 teaspoon each of peeled and grated fresh root ginger and garlic and chilli paste in a small bowl, and season with salt and pepper. Drizzle over the salad ingredients in the bowl. Toss gently to mix before serving.

bang bang chicken noodle salad

Serves **4**
Preparation time **15 minutes**,
  plus standing

250 g (8 oz) **dried fine rice
  vermicelli noodles**
4 cooked boneless **chicken
  breasts**, about 125 g (4 oz)
  each, skinned and roughly
  shredded
1 **cucumber**, halved,
  deseeded and cut into
  matchsticks
8 **spring onions**, thinly sliced
1 **red chilli**, thinly sliced
100 g (3½ oz) **reduced-fat
  smooth peanut butter**
6 tablespoons **light soy sauce**
2 tablespoons **white wine
  vinegar**
1 tablespoon **clear honey**
1 teaspoon **sesame oil**
1 teaspoon **chilli oil**
75 ml (3 fl oz) **warm water**
2 tablespoons **sesame seeds**,
  toasted

Place the noodles in a large heatproof bowl, pour
over boiling hot water to cover and leave to stand for
10 minutes, or until just tender. Drain and return to the
bowl. Add the chicken, cucumber, spring onions and
chilli, and toss to combine. Transfer to a serving bowl.

Stir together the peanut butter, soy sauce, vinegar,
honey, oils and 2 tablespoons of the measurement
water in a bowl until well combined. Gradually add the
remaining water to the sauce, stirring, until the sauce
reaches pouring consistency.

Drizzle the sauce over the salad. Sprinkle over the
sesame seeds and serve.

For chicken, prawn & lemon grass with noodles,
spray a large nonstick wok or frying pan with low-calorie
cooking spray and heat over a high heat. Add 500 g
(1 lb) minced chicken, 1 teaspoon each of peeled
and finely grated fresh root ginger and garlic, 1 finely
chopped red chilli and 1 tablespoon lemon grass paste
and stir-fry, breaking up the chicken with a wooden
spoon, for 3–4 minutes until the chicken is browned.
Stir in 300 g (10 oz) cooked peeled prawns and
1 tablespoon each of light soy sauce and fish sauce
and cook briefly, stirring, until heated through. Serve
immediately with noodles.

szechuan pickled cucumber

Serves **4**

Preparation time **10 minutes**, plus marinating

2 **cucumbers**

1 teaspoon **dried chilli flakes**

2 **spring onions**, finely chopped

1 **garlic clove**, crushed

½ teaspoon **soft light brown sugar**

5 teaspoons **light soy sauce**

2 teaspoons **sesame oil**

2 teaspoons **chilli oil**

¼ teaspoon **black rice vinegar**

½ teaspoon **sesame seeds**, toasted

Cut the cucumbers into finger-thick batons and place in a wide glass or ceramic bowl.

Mix together all the remaining ingredients in a small bowl and pour over the cucumber. Toss to mix well. Cover and leave to marinate at room temperature for 1 hour.

Spoon on to small plates and serve with rice.

For Szechuan stir-fried cucumbers with hot chilli oil, deseed and thinly slice 3 large cucumbers into thin batons. Heat 2 tablespoons groundnut oil in a large nonstick wok or frying pan until smoking. Add 1 tablespoon crushed Szechuan peppercorns and the cucumber and stir-fry for 1–2 minutes. Drizzle in 2 tablespoons light soy sauce and cook, stirring, for 30–40 seconds. Remove from the heat and drizzle over 2 tablespoons chilli oil. Serve immediately with rice.

peanut, squid & noodle salad

Serves **4**

Preparation time **25 minutes**, plus standing

Cooking time **15 minutes**

175 g (6 oz) **dried fine rice noodles**

500 g (1 lb) cleaned **baby squid**

3 **red chillies**, deseeded and finely chopped

3 **garlic cloves**, finely chopped

2 tablespoons chopped **coriander**, plus extra leaves to serve

3 tablespoons **groundnut oil**

175 g (6 oz) **unsalted peanuts**, roughly chopped

125 g (4 oz) **green beans**, roughly chopped

3 tablespoons **fish sauce**

1 teaspoon **caster sugar**

3 tablespoons **lemon juice**

3 tablespoons **water**

Place the noodles in a large heatproof bowl, pour over boiling hot water to cover and leave to stand for 5–8 minutes, or according to the packet instructions, until just tender. Drain well and rinse under cold running water.

Cut the squid bodies in half lengthways and use a sharp knife to make a series of slashes in a diagonal crisscross pattern on the underside of each piece.

Mix together the chillies, garlic and chopped coriander in a glass or ceramic bowl. Add the squid pieces and toss in the mixture, then leave to stand for about 20 minutes.

Heat the oil in a nonstick wok or large frying pan over a medium heat. Add the peanuts and stir-fry for about 2–3 minutes until golden brown. Remove with a slotted spoon and set aside. Add the squid to the pan and stir-fry for 2–3 minutes, or until beginning to curl and turn white. Set aside with the peanuts.

Add the green beans to the pan and stir-fry for 2 minutes. Stir in the fish sauce, sugar, lemon juice and measurement water and cook for a further minute. Remove the pan from the heat, add the drained noodles and toss together. Add the peanuts, squid and extra coriander leaves and toss again. Serve warm or cool with lime wedges, if liked.

spicy sui mai dumplings

Makes **36**
Preparation time **30 minutes**
Cooking time **6–8 minutes**

150 g (5 oz) **minced pork**
100 g (3½ oz) **raw peeled tiger prawns**, very finely chopped
2 **spring onions**, finely chopped
1 **red chilli**, finely chopped
2 **garlic cloves**, crushed
2 teaspoons peeled and finely grated **fresh root ginger**
2 tablespoons **oyster sauce**
1 teaspoon **sesame oil**
5 canned **water chestnuts**, rinsed, drained and finely chopped
36 **fresh wonton wrappers**

Dipping sauce
2 tablespoons **dark soy sauce**
2 tablespoons **Shaoxing rice wine**
2 teaspoons peeled and finely chopped **fresh root ginger**
1 **red chilli**, finely chopped

Mix together the pork, prawns, spring onions, chilli, garlic, ginger, oyster sauce, sesame oil and water chestnuts with your fingers in a bowl until well combined.

Lay a wonton wrapper in the palm of one hand. Place 1 teaspoonful of the pork mixture in the centre. Dampen the wrapper edges with water and bring up the sides, then press them around the filling, leaving the filling exposed. Gently tap on the work surface to create a flat base. Repeat with the remaining wrappers and pork mixture. (You can refrigerate on a tray lined with nonstick baking paper for up to 1 hour before cooking.)

Combine all the ingredients for the sauce in a small bowl.

Place the dumplings without touching in stacking bamboo steamer baskets lined with nonstick baking paper, cover and steam over a wok or large saucepan of boiling water (see page 14) for 6–8 minutes until cooked through. If you don't have stacking baskets, steam in 2 batches. Transfer the cooked batch to a heatproof plate, cover loosely with foil and keep hot over a saucepan of simmering water while cooking the second batch.

Serve the dumplings with the sauce for dipping.

For prawn & chive dumplings, follow the recipe above to prepare the filling mixture, omitting the minced pork, using 300 g (10 oz) raw peeled tiger prawns and replacing the red chilli with 1 tablespoon very finely chopped Chinese chives. Make the dumplings and steam until cooked through as above, then serve with homemade Sweet Chilli Dipping Sauce (see page 26).

chilli crab on noodle nests

Makes **20**
Preparation time **10 minutes**,
 plus cooling
Cooking time **15 minutes**

100 g (3½ oz) **fresh fine egg
 noodles**
1 tablespoon **sunflower oil**,
 plus extra for greasing and
 brushing
2 **spring onions**, thinly sliced
2 **garlic cloves**, finely chopped
1 teaspoon peeled and finely
 chopped **fresh root ginger**
1 **red chilli**, deseeded and
 finely chopped
200 g (7 oz) **fresh white
 crabmeat**
2 tablespoons **sweet chilli
 sauce**
4 tablespoons finely chopped
 coriander

Grease a 20-hole nonstick mini tartlet tin lightly with oil. Divide the noodles into 20 portions and press each portion into a tartlet case to form a tartlet shape, making sure the base is covered. Lightly brush with more oil and bake in a preheated oven, 180°C (350°F), Gas Mark 4, for 8–10 minutes, or until crisp and firm. Remove from the cases and leave to cool on a wire rack.

Heat the 1 tablespoon oil in a large nonstick wok or frying pan, add the spring onions, garlic, ginger and chilli and stir-fry for 2–3 minutes. Add the crabmeat and stir-fry for a further 1–2 minutes, then remove from the heat, stir in the sweet chilli sauce and coriander and toss to mix well.

Place 1 heaped teaspoon of the chilli crab mixture into each cooled noodle nest and serve immediately.

For chilli crab linguine, cook 300 g (10 oz) dried linguine in a large saucepan of lightly salted boiling water for about 10 minutes, or according to the packet instructions, then drain. Meanwhile, heat 2 tablespoons olive oil in a large frying pan, add 1 finely chopped large red chilli and stir-fry for 2 minutes. Stir in 4 thinly sliced spring onions, 375 g (12 oz) fresh white crabmeat, the juice of 1 lime and 2 tablespoons roughly chopped coriander leaves and warm through. Add the drained linguine and toss all the ingredients together. Dress the crab linguine with 2 tablespoons olive oil and serve immediately.

hot & sour soup with tofu

Serves **4**
Preparation time **20 minutes**
Cooking time **25 minutes**

1.2 litres (2 pints) **vegetable**
  or **chicken stock**
300 g (10 oz) **mixed**
  mushrooms, trimmed and
  sliced
50 g (2 oz) canned sliced
  bamboo shoots, rinsed and
  drained
1 teaspoon peeled and grated
  fresh root ginger
2 **garlic cloves,** crushed
1 tablespoon **soy sauce**
¼ teaspoon **dried chilli flakes**
1 tablespoon **cornflour**
3 tablespoons **white wine**
  vinegar
1 **egg**, beaten
4 **spring onions**, chopped
small handful of chopped
  coriander
200 g (7 oz) **firm tofu**, drained
  and cut into bite-sized cubes

To garnish
shredded **spring onions**
thinly sliced **red chilli**

Combine the stock, mushrooms, bamboo shoots, ginger, garlic, soy sauce and chilli flakes in a saucepan. Bring to the boil, then reduce the heat to low, cover and simmer for about 15 minutes while you assemble the rest of the ingredients.

Mix the cornflour with the vinegar in a small bowl until smooth, then set aside.

Return the soup to a rolling boil. Drizzle in the beaten egg while stirring slowly to create long strands. Stir in the spring onions, coriander and cornflour mixture. Reduce the heat and simmer, stirring occcaisonally, for about 3 minutes until the stock has thickened slightly.

Stir in the tofu and cook briefly until heated through. Serve the soup garnished with shredded spring onions and red chilli slices.

For hot tofu & spring onion stir-fry, spray a nonstick wok or large frying pan with low-calorie cooking spray and heat over a high heat. Add 3 crushed garlic cloves and 1 teaspoon peeled and grated fresh root ginger and stir-fry for 10–20 seconds, then add 12 thickly sliced spring onions, 500 g (1 lb) firm tofu, drained and cut into bite-sized cubes, and 1 diced red chilli. Stir-fry for 4–5 minutes until the tofu is lightly browned. Add 100 ml (3½ fl oz) vegetable stock and 2 tablespoons dark soy sauce and cook over a medium heat for 6–8 minutes until all the liquid is absorbed. Serve immediately with egg noodles or rice.

pot sticker dumplings

Serves **4**

Preparation time **40 minutes**, plus resting

Cooking time **20 minutes**

1 tablespoon **groundnut oil**

100 ml (3½ fl oz) **boiling water**

sweet chilli dipping sauce (see page 26), to serve

Dumpling dough

150 g (5 oz) **plain flour**, plus extra for dusting

125 ml (4 fl oz) **boiling water**

Filling

60 g (2¼ oz) **raw peeled tiger prawns**, finely chopped

60 g (2¼ oz) **minced pork**

4 **spring onions**, very finely chopped

1 teaspoon peeled and grated **fresh root ginger**

½ tablespoon **Shaoxing rice wine**

1 tablespoon **dark soy sauce**, plus extra to serve

¼ teaspoon ground **white pepper**

Place the flour for the dough in a mixing bowl and, using a fork, gradually stir in the measurement water until incorporated. Add more water if the mixture seems dry.

Transfer the dough to a clean work surface and knead for 8–10 minutes, dusting with a little flour if sticky. Return to the bowl, cover with a damp tea towel and leave to rest for 20 minutes.

Mix all the ingredients for the filling together in a separate bowl until well combined. Set aside.

Knead the dough again for 5–6 minutes until smooth, then shape into a roll about 23 cm (9 inches) long, 2.5 cm (1 inch) in diameter, then slice into 16 pieces. Roll each piece into a small ball, then roll out each ball into a 9 cm (3½ inch) 'pancake'. Cover them with a damp tea towel to prevent them from drying out. Place 2 teaspoons of filling in the centre of each 'pancake' and moisten the edges with water. Fold the dough in half to form a moon shape and pinch the edges together with your fingers. Pleat around the edge, pinching to seal well.

Heat the groundnut oil in a large, lidded nonstick frying pan until very hot and add the dumplings. Reduce the heat and cook for 2 minutes until lightly browned. Add the measurement water, cover the pan and simmer gently for 12–15 minutes, or until most of the liquid is absorbed. Check halfway through and add more water if necessary. Uncover and cook for a further 2–3 minutes. Serve with dark soy sauce and sweet chilli sauce for dipping.

For chilli beef pot sticker dumplings, prepare the dumpling dough as above. For the filling, replace the prawns and pork with 125 g (4 oz) minced beef and add 2 finely chopped red chillies. Continue as above.

baked vegetable spring rolls

Serves **4**
Preparation time **25 minutes**,
  plus soaking and cooling
Cooking time **15–20 minutes**

16 **dried Chinese mushrooms**
low-calorie cooking spray
1 tablespoon **light soy sauce**
2 teaspoons **Chinese five-**
  spice powder
100 g (3½ oz) **bean sprouts**
4 **spring onions**, finely
  chopped
1 small **carrot**, finely chopped
1 teaspoon peeled and grated
  fresh root ginger
2 tablespoons **oyster sauce**
16 **spring roll wrappers**,
  thawed if frozen
1 tablespoon **cornflour**,
  mixed to a paste with
  2 tablespoons **cold water**
1 **egg yolk**, beaten
salt and **white pepper**
sweet chilli dipping sauce
  (see page 26), to serve

Place the dried mushrooms in a heatproof bowl, pour over boiling hot water and leave to soak for 30 minutes until softened. Drain and squeeze out the excess water. Remove and discard the stems, and finely chop the caps.

Spray a large wok or frying pan with cooking spray and heat until smoking. Add the mushrooms and stir-fry for 1–2 minutes, then stir in the soy sauce and five-spice powder. Remove from the pan and leave to cool for 10 minutes. Wipe the pan clean with kitchen paper.

Place the bean sprouts, spring onions, carrot and ginger in a bowl, add the mushroom mixture and oyster sauce and season well with salt and white pepper. Mix well.

Lay 2 spring roll wrappers on top of each other. Spoon 2 tablespoons of the filling in the centre. Brush each corner with cornflour paste. Fold the 2 opposite corners over the filling, then roll the wrapper up tightly from one of the other corners. Seal the roll with a little beaten egg yolk. Repeat with the remaining wrappers and filling.

Arrange the rolls on a baking sheet lined with nonstick baking paper, lightly spray with cooking spray and bake in a preheated oven, 200°C (400°F), Gas Mark 6, for 12–15 minutes, or until lightly golden and crisp. Serve immediately with sweet chilli sauce for dipping.

For mushroom & bean sprout stir-fry, spray a large nonstick wok with cooking spray and heat over a high heat. Add 400 g (13 oz) sliced shiitake mushrooms, 1 teaspoon each of grated fresh root ginger and garlic and stir-fry for 6–8 minutes. Add 1 finely chopped carrot, 6 sliced spring onions and 100 g (3½ oz) beansprouts and stir-fry for a further 3–4 minutes before serving.

egg drop soup

Serves **4**
Preparation time **10 minutes**
Cooking time **10 minutes**

1.2 litres (2 pints) **chicken stock**
2 tablespoons **cornflour** mixed to a paste with 3 tablespoons **cold water**
2 tablespoons **dark soy sauce**
1 tablespoon **white wine vinegar**
6 **spring onions**, thinly sliced
3 **eggs**, beaten
chilli oil, for drizzling
sliced spring onions, to garnish

Place the stock in a saucepan and bring to the boil.

Stir the cornflour and water mixture into the stock. Add the soy sauce, vinegar and spring onions. Return to the boil, then reduce the heat and simmer, stirring occasionally, for about 3 minutes until the stock has thickened slightly.

Pour the beaten eggs gradually into the soup while stirring vigorously until just set in strands.

Remove the pan from the heat, ladle the soup into warmed bowls, drizzle with chilli oil and serve.

For prawn & Chinese chive soup, bring 1.2 litres (2 pints) fish stock to the boil in a saucepan. Mix 2 tablespoons cornflour to a paste with 3 tablespoons cold water, then stir into the stock. Stir in 2 tablespoons light soy sauce, a handful of finely chopped Chinese chives, 400 g (13 oz) raw peeled tiger prawns and 2 thinly sliced spring onions. Return to the boil, then simmer, stirring occasionally, for about 5 minutes until the mixture has thickened slightly and the prawns have turned pink and are firm. Gradually pour in 2 beaten eggs while stirring vigorously until just set in strands. Remove the pan from the heat, ladle the soup into warmed bowls and serve immediately.

crayfish rolls with hoisin sauce

Serves **4**
Preparation time **25 minutes**,
  plus soaking
Cooking time **1 minute**

8 **rice paper sheets**
16 **long chives**
4 **iceberg lettuce leaves**,
  finely shredded
4 **spring onions**, finely
  shredded into matchsticks
16 **mint leaves**, shredded
16 **cooked peeled crayfish
  tails**
3 tablespoons **hoisin sauce**,
  to serve

Fill a shallow bowl with hot water and soak the rice paper sheets for about 5 minutes until softened. Remove the sheets from the water and place on a clean, dry tea towel. Cut in half.

Blanch the chives in a saucepan of boiling water for 10 seconds, then drain and cool under cold running water.

Lay 1 half-sheet of rice paper on a clean work surface and fill with a little lettuce, spring onions, mint and a crayfish tail. Roll up the rice paper sheet to enclose the ingredients, folding in the ends as you go. Tie a chive around the centre of the roll to seal it closed, then place on a tray and cover with a clean, damp tea towel while making the remaining rolls.

Serve the crayfish rolls with the hoisin sauce for dipping.

For prawn & bamboo shoot spring rolls, brush 1 sheet of filo pastry with a little melted butter. With the short side of the pastry in line with your body, place 1 raw peeled king prawn and a small pile of canned bamboo shoots, rinsed and drained, in the centre of the pastry at the edge. Roll up the filo pastry sheet to enclose the ingredients, folding in the ends as you go. Repeat with 15 more sheets of filo pastry, 15 more prawns and some bamboo shoots. Brush the spring rolls with melted butter and bake in a preheated oven, 180°C (350°F), Gas Mark 4, for 10–15 minutes until golden brown. Serve with hoisin sauce for dipping.

prawn & pork wonton soup

Serves **4**
Preparation time **25 minutes**
Cooking time **5–6 minutes**

100 g (3½ oz) **minced pork**
150 g (5 oz) **raw peeled prawns**
4 **spring onions**, finely chopped
1 **garlic clove**, peeled
1 cm (½ inch) piece of **fresh root ginger**, chopped
1 tablespoon **oyster sauce**
20 **fresh wonton wrappers**
750 ml (1¼ pints) **chicken stock**
1 head of **Chinese spring greens**, shredded
1–2 tablespoons **fish sauce**

To serve
leaves from a small bunch of **coriander**
1 tablespoon **sesame seeds**

Place the pork, prawns, 2 of the spring onions, the garlic, ginger and oyster sauce in a food processor and process to a paste.

Spoon 1 teaspoon of the pork mixture in the centre of a wonton wrapper. Dampen the edges with water, bring up the sides around the filling and pinch the edges together to seal. Repeat with the remaining wrappers and pork mixture. (You can refrigerate, covered with clingfilm, for up to 12 hours before cooking.)

Bring the stock to the boil in a large saucepan, then reduce the heat, add the wontons and simmer for 4–5 minutes. Remove a wonton and check that it has become firm, which will indicate that it is cooked.

Add the spring greens to the pan and cook for 1 minute. Season the stock with the fish sauce. Divide the soup between 4 warmed bowls and serve with a few coriander leaves and a sprinkling of sesame seeds.

For sesame wontons with soy dipping sauce,
follow the recipe above to make the wontons. Place without touching in stacking bamboo steamer baskets lined with baking paper, cover and steam (see page 14) for 5 minutes until cooked through. If you don't have stacking baskets, steam in 2 batches and keep the cooked batch hot over a saucepan of simmering water while cooking the second batch. Meanwhile, make a dipping sauce by mixing together 3 tablespoons light soy sauce, 2 teaspoons grated fresh root ginger, 1 thinly sliced red chilli and 1 tablespoon fish sauce in a small bowl. Sprinkle 2 tablespoons sesame seeds over the wontons and serve with the dipping sauce.

black bean soup with soba

Serves **4**

Preparation time **10 minutes**

Cooking time **8 minutes**

200 g (7 oz) **dried soba noodles**

2 tablespoons **groundnut** or **vegetable oil**

1 bunch of **spring onions**, sliced

2 **garlic cloves**, roughly chopped

1 **red chilli**, deseeded and sliced

3.5 cm (1½ inch) piece of **fresh root ginger**, peeled and grated

125 ml (4 fl oz) **black bean sauce** or **black bean stir-fry sauce**

750 ml (1¼ pints) **vegetable stock**

200 g (7 oz) **pak choi** or **spring greens**, shredded

2 teaspoons **light soy sauce**

1 teaspoon **caster sugar**

50 g (2 oz) **raw unsalted peanuts**

Cook the noodles in a large saucepan of boiling water for about 5 minutes, or according to the packet instructions, until just tender.

Meanwhile, heat the oil in a saucepan over a medium heat, add the spring onions and garlic and stir-fry for 1 minute. Add the chilli, ginger, black bean sauce and stock and bring to the boil.

Stir the pak choi or spring greens, soy sauce, sugar and peanuts into the soup, then reduce the heat and simmer gently for 4 minutes.

Drain the noodles, rinse with fresh hot water and spoon into 4 warmed bowls. Ladle the soup over the top and serve immediately.

For chicken & black bean soup, follow the recipe above to cook the noodles. Meanwhile, heat the oil in a saucepan, add 3 boneless, skinless chicken thighs, chopped into small chunks, and fry for 4–5 minutes, or until cooked through. Add the spring onions and garlic and continue with the recipe above, replacing the vegetable stock with 750 ml (1¼ pints) chicken stock and omitting the peanuts.

meat

beef & black bean stir-fry

Serves **4**
Preparation time **15 minutes**,
plus marinating
Cooking time **15 minutes**

200 ml (7 fl oz) **black bean sauce**

2 tablespoons **Shaoxing rice wine**

2 **garlic cloves**, crushed

500 g (1 lb) lean **beef fillet steak**, thinly sliced

low-calorie cooking spray

1 **onion**, cut into wedges

200 g (7 oz) **sugar snap peas**, trimmed

1 **red pepper**, cored, deseeded and thinly sliced

Combine the black bean sauce, rice wine and garlic in a bowl. Place the beef in a glass or ceramic bowl, add half the sauce mixture and toss to coat evenly. Cover and leave to marinate in the refrigerator for 3–4 hours.

Spray a nonstick wok or frying pan with cooking spray and heat over a high heat. Add the beef and stir-fry for 4–5 minutes, or until just cooked. Transfer to a bowl.

Wipe the pan clean with kitchen paper, re-spray with cooking spray and heat over a high heat. Add the onion and stir-fry for about 1–2 minutes until slightly softened. Add the sugar snap peas and red pepper and stir-fry for about 2–3 minutes until just tender.

Return the beef to the pan, add the remaining sauce mixture and cook, stirring, for about 1 minute until heated through. Serve with steamed jasmine rice.

For pork, baby mushroom & black bean stir-fry, follow the recipe above, replacing the beef with 500 g (1 lb) lean pork steaks, cut into thin strips, and using 200 g (7 oz) baby button mushrooms, trimmed and halved, instead of the sugar snap peas.

roast char siu pork

Serves **4**
Preparation time **20 minutes**,
    plus marinating and resting
Cooking time **45 minutes**

625 g (1¼ lb) lean **pork
    tenderloin fillet**
4 **garlic cloves**, crushed
2 tablespoons peeled and
    grated **fresh root ginger**
1 teaspoon **Chinese
    five-spice powder**
100 ml (3½ fl oz) **light soy
    sauce**
4 tablespoons **Shaoxing rice
    wine**
3 tablespoons **soft light
    brown sugar**
2 tablespoons **hoisin sauce**
2 tablespoons **sweet chilli
    sauce**
2 tablespoons **clear honey**
1 tablespoon **groundnut oil**

Make deep slashes all over the pork with a sharp knife and place in a shallow glass or ceramic dish. Mix together all the remaining ingredients and spread all over the pork, rubbing it into the slashes. Cover and leave to marinate in the refrigerator for 3–4 hours, or overnight if time permits.

Place a roasting rack or wire rack over a roasting tin. Pour hot water into the tin to come halfway up the sides. Remove the pork from marinade, reserving the marinade, and lay on the rack. Place in a preheated oven, 200°C (400°F), Gas Mark 6, and roast for 20 minutes.

Turn the pork over and brush well with some of the marinade. Reduce the oven temperature to 180°C (350°F), Gas Mark 4, and roast for a further 20 minutes. Remove from the oven, cover with foil and leave to rest for 10–15 minutes.

Meanwhile, place the remaining marinade in a small saucepan and bring to the boil.

Slice the pork thinly and serve with the extra marinade, together with egg noodles and steamed Asian greens.

For quick char siu pork fried rice, spray a large nonstick wok or frying pan with low-calorie cooking spray and heat over a high heat. Add 2 teaspoons each of finely chopped fresh root ginger and garlic and stir-fry for 30 seconds. Add 625 g (1¼ lb) lean minced pork and stir-fry for 3–4 minutes. Add 4 tablespoons char siu sauce (Chinese barbecue sauce), 2 tablespoons light soy sauce and 500 g (1 lb) cooled freshly cooked jasmine or long-grain rice and toss together for 5–6 minutes until piping hot. Serve immediately with steamed Asian greens.

lamb & green bean stir-fry

Serves **4**
Preparation time **15 minutes**
Cooking time **10 minutes**

500 g (1 lb) boneless lean
   lamb leg steaks, cut into
   2.5 cm (1 inch) pieces
3 **garlic cloves**, crushed
1 tablespoon peeled and
   grated **fresh root ginger**
1 tablespoon **Chinese
   five-spice powder**
1 teaspoon **dried chilli flakes**
4 tablespoons **light soy sauce**
low-calorie cooking spray
1 **onion**, cut into wedges
300 g (10 oz) **green beans**,
   trimmed
2 tablespoons **kecap manis**
small handful of **mint leaves**

To garnish
chilli slivers
cucumber ribbons

Combine the lamb, garlic, ginger, five-spice powder, chilli flakes and 2 tablespoons of the soy sauce in a bowl.

Spray a large nonstick wok or frying pan with cooking spray and heat over a high heat until just smoking. Add the onion and green beans and stir-fry for about 3–4 minutes until lightly charred and tender. Transfer to a bowl.

Wipe the pan clean with kitchen paper, re-spray with cooking spray and heat over a high heat. Add half the lamb mixture and stir-fry for 2 minutes, or until browned and just cooked through. Transfer to a plate. Wipe the pan clean, spray again with cooking spray and stir-fry the rest of the lamb mixture in the same way.

Return all the lamb mixture to the pan with the onion mixture and add the remaining soy sauce and the kecap manis. Cook, stirring, for about 30 seconds until heated through.

Divide between 4 warmed bowls, garnish with chilli slivers and cucumber ribbons and serve with egg noodles.

For quick prawn & green bean stir-fry, follow the recipe above, replacing the lamb with 625 g (1 ¼ lb) raw peeled tiger prawns. After stir-frying the onion and green beans as above, add the prawn mixture to the pan and continue to stir-fry for 4–5 minutes until the prawns have turned pink and are firm. Remove from the heat and garnish with chopped coriander before serving with noodles or rice.

grilled hoisin pork

Serves **4**
Preparation time **15 minutes**,
  plus marinating
Cooking time **10–12 minutes**

8 boneless lean **pork loin
  steaks**, about 100 g (3½ oz)
  each
4 tablespoons **hoisin sauce**
3 tablespoons **dark soy sauce**
4 **garlic cloves**, crushed
2 teaspoons peeled and finely
  grated **fresh root ginger**
1 teaspoon **Szechuan
  peppercorns**, crushed
2 tablespoons **tomato purée**
2 tablespoons **cider vinegar**

To garnish
4 **spring onions**, finely
  shredded
1 **red chilli**, deseeded and
  finely shredded

Place the pork steaks in a shallow glass or ceramic dish in a single layer. Mix together the hoisin sauce, soy sauce, garlic, ginger, crushed Szechuan peppercorns, tomato purée and vinegar, then brush or spoon the mixture on to the pork. Cover and leave to marinate in the refrigerator for 2–3 hours.

Arrange the pork on a grill rack in a single layer and cook under a preheated medium-high grill for 5–6 minutes on each side, or until cooked through.

Remove from the grill, garnish with the spring onions and red chilli and serve with steamed rice and steamed Asian greens.

For grilled sweet chilli pork chops, place 4 large lean pork chops, about 175g (6 oz) each, in a glass or ceramic dish in a single layer. Mix together 6 tablespoons sweet chilli sauce, the juice of 1 lime, 2 teaspoons each of peeled and grated fresh root ginger, garlic and light soy sauce. Spoon over the pork chops and toss to coat evenly. Cover and leave to marinate in the refrigerator for 1–2 hours, or overnight if time permits. Arrange the chops on a grill rack and cook under preheated a medium-high grill for 5–6 minutes on each side, or until cooked through. Serve with a mixed vegetable salad.

char siu beef with broccoli

Serves **4**
Preparation time **15 minutes**
Cooking time **10 minutes**

300 g (10 oz) **tenderstem broccoli**, thinly sliced
low-calorie cooking spray
2 **garlic cloves**, finely chopped
1 tablespoon peeled and grated **fresh root ginger**
500 g (1 lb) lean **minced beef steak**
4 tablespoons **Shaoxing rice wine**
6 tablespoons **char siu sauce** (Chinese barbecue sauce)
50 g (2 oz) **roasted peanuts**, roughly chopped
1 **red chilli**, deseeded and thinly sliced

Blanch the broccoli in a saucepan of boiling water for 1–2 minutes. Drain and set aside.

Spray a large nonstick wok or frying pan with cooking spray and heat over a high heat. Add the garlic, ginger and minced beef and stir-fry, breaking up the beef with a wooden spoon, for 3–4 minutes until the meat is browned.

Add the rice wine and char siu sauce and simmer for 1 minute. Add the broccoli and cook, stirring, for 1–2 minutes until heated through.

Remove the pan from the heat and scatter over the peanuts and chilli. Serve with rice noodles.

For hoisin beef with peas, spray a large nonstick wok or frying pan with low-calorie cooking spray and heat over a high heat. Add the garlic, ginger and minced beef and stir-fry for 3–4 minutes as in the recipe above. Add the rice wine as above with 6 tablespoons hoisin sauce and simmer for 1–2 minutes. Stir in 200 g (7 oz) fresh or frozen peas and cook for 3–4 minutes until just tender. Stir in a handful of chopped mint and serve with noodles.

pork with honey & ginger

Serves **4**
Preparation time **15 minutes**,
plus marinating
Cooking time **10 minutes**

500 g (1 lb) lean **pork**, thinly
sliced
1 teaspoon **cornflour**
2 teaspoons peeled and finely
chopped **fresh root ginger**
2 tablespoons **dark soy sauce**
2 tablespoons **clear honey**
2 tablespoons **Shaoxing rice
wine**
2 teaspoons **Chinese
five-spice powder**
1 teaspoon **sesame oil**
3 tablespoons **groundnut oil**
1 **green pepper**, cored,
deseeded and cubed
3 **spring onions**, cut into 5 cm
(2 inch) lengths
1 tablespoon **malt vinegar**
1 tablespoon **light soy sauce**
2 tablespoons **water**
squeeze of **lime juice**
salt and **white pepper**

Place the pork in a bowl and sprinkle over the cornflour. Add the ginger, dark soy sauce, honey, rice wine, Chinese five-spice powder and sesame oil and toss to coat evenly. Cover and leave to marinate at room temperature for 30 minutes, or up to overnight in the refrigerator, then drain the pork.

Heat half the groundnut oil in a nonstick wok or large frying pan over a high heat until the oil starts to shimmer. Add half the pork and stir-fry for 2 minutes, then remove with a slotted spoon. Wipe the pan clean with kitchen paper. Heat the remaining oil in the pan and stir-fry the rest of the pork in the same way.

Return all the pork to the pan, add the green pepper, spring onions, vinegar, light soy sauce and measurement water and cook, stirring, for a further 3 minutes until the pork is well browned and the pepper has softened slightly.

Season with salt and white pepper to taste, then add the lime juice. Serve with rice and lime wedges, if liked.

For mussels with honey & ginger, follow the recipe above, replacing the pork with 1 kg (2 lb) scrubbed and debearded live mussels (see page 150), discarding any open ones that do not close when tapped, and omitting the cornflour. Heat 1 tablespoon groundnut oil in a wok or large frying pan over a high heat. Add the ginger as above and stir-fry for a few seconds, then add the dark soy sauce, honey, rice wine and sesame oil. Bring to the boil, tip in the mussels and simmer, covered, for 2–3 minutes until opened, discarding any that remain closed. Stir in the spring onions, light soy sauce and lime juice and serve immediately.

red braised lamb

Serves **4–6**
Preparation time **15 minutes**
Cooking time **about 3 hours**

875 g (1¾ lb) boneless lean
   lamb shoulder, cut into
   bite-sized cubes
thumb-sized piece of **fresh
   root ginger,** peeled and cut
   into matchsticks
4 **garlic cloves,** chopped
1 **onion,** sliced
1 teaspoon **Chinese
   five-spice powder**
1 **star anise**
1 **cinnamon stick**
1 teaspoon **black
   peppercorns,** crushed
2 **cardamom pods,** crushed
1 tablespoon **tomato purée**
6 tablespoons **Shaoxing rice
   wine**
3 tablespoons **dark soy sauce**
2 tablespoons **light soy sauce**
3 tablespoons **soft dark
   brown sugar**
500 ml (17 fl oz) **water** or
   chicken stock

To garnish
sliced **spring onions**
sliced **red chillies**

Place all the ingredients in a heavy-based flameproof
casserole dish with a tight-fitting lid, pouring over the
measurement water or stock at the end. Bring to a
simmer on the hob.

Cover the casserole dish and transfer to a preheated
oven, 150°C (300°F), Gas Mark 2, for about 3 hours
until the lamb is meltingly tender.

Remove the casserole dish from the oven and garnish
the lamb with sliced spring onions and red chillies.
Serve with egg noodles or rice.

For Chinese-style lamb burgers, place 875 g (1¾ lb)
lean minced lamb in a bowl with 2 teaspoons each
of grated garlic and peeled fresh root ginger, 2 finely
chopped spring onions, 2 teaspoons Chinese five-spice
powder and 1 tablespoon each of light soy sauce and
sweet chilli sauce. Season with salt and pepper and
mix with your fingers until well combined. Cover and
chill in the refrigerator for 1–2 hours, or overnight if
time permits. Divide the mixture into 8 portions and
form each one into a burger. Cook under a preheated
medium-high grill for 4–5 minutes on each side, or until
cooked to your liking. Serve with a chopped mixed salad.

hoisin pork, rice & greens

Serves **4**
Preparation time **15 minutes**,
  plus marinating
Cooking time **20–25 minutes**

200 g (7 oz) **easy-cook
  basmati rice**
3 tablespoons **hoisin sauce**
2 **garlic cloves**, crushed
5 cm (2 inch) piece of **fresh
  root ginger**, peeled and
  grated
1 **red chilli**, deseeded and
  sliced
1 **star anise**
1 tablespoon **sun-dried
  tomato purée**
300 g (10 oz) lean **pork
  tenderloin fillet**, cut into
  thin strips
low-calorie cooking spray
1 **red onion**, chopped
125 g (4 oz) **cabbage** or
  spring greens, finely
  chopped
1 **carrot**, thinly sliced
salt
toasted sesame seeds, to
  serve

Cook the rice in a saucepan of salted boiling water for 16–18 minutes until just tender. Drain and set aside.

Meanwhile, mix together the hoisin sauce, garlic, ginger, chilli, star anise and tomato purée in a bowl. Add the pork and toss to coat evenly. Cover and leave to marinate in a cool place for up to 1 hour, then drain the pork.

Spray a nonstick wok or large frying pan with cooking spray and heat over a high heat. Add the pork and stir-fry for about 2 minutes until browned and cooked through. Stir in the onion, cabbage or spring greens and carrot, followed by the rice. Toss together for about 3 minutes until the rice is piping hot. Sprinkle with toasted sesame seeds and serve immediately.

For hoisin lamb with stir-fry noodles, follow the recipe above, omitting the rice, replacing the pork with 300 g (10 oz) lamb fillet and omitting the tomato purée. Marinate and then stir-fry the lamb and the vegetables as above. Add 3 x 150 g (5 oz) packets straight-to-wok rice noodles (or dried rice noodles, cooked according to the packet instructions) to the pan and toss together for about 1 minute until heated through. Sprinkle with chopped coriander leaves instead of sesame seeds to serve.

braised beef in ginger & garlic

Serves **4**
Preparation time **25 minutes**
Cooking time **2¼ hours**

low-calorie cooking spray
750 g (1½ lb) lean **stewing beef**, cut into bite-sized pieces
2 **onions**, thickly sliced
2 tablespoons peeled and grated **fresh root ginger**
4 **garlic cloves**, crushed
2 teaspoons **Chinese five-spice powder**
4 **star anise**
1 **cinnamon stick**
1 **dried red chilli**
10 **black peppercorns**
2 tablespoons **soft light brown sugar**
7 tablespoons **light soy sauce**
4 tablespoons **tomato purée**
750 ml (1¼ pints) **rich beef stock**

Spray a large flameproof casserole dish with a tightly fitting lid with cooking spray and heat over a high heat. Add half the beef and stir-fry for about 5–6 minutes until browned. Transfer to a plate with a slotted spoon. Re-spray the casserole with cooking spray, stir-fry the rest of the beef in the same way and transfer to the plate.

Wipe the casserole clean with kitchen paper, spray again lightly with cooking spray and heat over a medium heat. Add the onions, ginger, garlic and spices and stir-fry for 1 minute, then add the sugar, soy sauce and tomato purée. Return the beef and any juices to the casserole, then stir in the stock to just about cover and bring to a gentle simmer.

Cover the casserole tightly, transfer to a preheated oven, 160°C (325°F), Gas Mark 3, and cook for 2 hours, or until the beef is meltingly tender.

Serve in warmed bowls with steamed rice.

For beef, ginger & garlic stir-fry, spray a nonstick wok or large frying pan with low-calorie cooking spray and heat over a high heat. Add 6 sliced spring onions, 2 tablespoons peeled and grated fresh root ginger and 4 finely chopped garlic cloves and stir-fry for 30 seconds. Add 500 g (1 lb) thinly sliced lean sirloin steak and stir-fry for 2–3 minutes, or until just cooked and sealed. Stir in a large handful of bean sprouts, 6 tablespoons oyster sauce and 75 ml (3 fl oz) beef stock. Cook, stirring, over a high heat for 3–4 minutes until bubbling. Remove from the heat and serve with steamed rice.

mu shu pork

Serves **4**

Preparation time **15 minutes**

Cooking time **10 minutes**

low-calorie cooking spray

625 g (1¼ lb) lean **minced pork**

2 **garlic cloves**, crushed

2 teaspoons peeled and grated **fresh root ginger**

6 tablespoons **light soy sauce**

3 tablespoons **oyster sauce**

2 tablespoons **Shaoxing rice wine**

1 **carrot**, cut into matchsticks

1 **red pepper**, cored, deseeded and thinly sliced

100 g (3½ oz) **shiitake mushrooms**, thinly sliced

6 **spring onions**, thinly sliced diagonally, plus extra to garnish

200 g (7 oz) **Chinese cabbage**, finely shredded

2 teaspoons **sesame oil**

Spray a large nonstick wok or frying pan with cooking spray and heat over a high heat. Add the pork and stir-fry, breaking it up with a wooden spoon, for about 2–3 minutes until browned. Transfer to a bowl. Add the soy sauce, oyster sauce and rice wine to the pork in the bowl.

Wipe the pan clean with kitchen paper, re-spray with cooking spray and heat over a high heat. Add the carrot, red pepper and mushrooms and stir-fry for 2–3 minutes until softened, then add the spring onions, cabbage and pork mixture and stir-fry for 2–3 minutes until the cabbage has just wilted.

Remove the pan from the heat, stir in the sesame oil and serve immediately, garnished with sliced spring onion.

For mu shu pork fried rice, follow the recipe above, replacing the cabbage with 500 g (1 lb) cooled freshly cooked jasmine or long-grain rice. Once added to the pan, stir-fry for 4–5 minutes until piping hot. Remove the pan from the heat and stir in 4 tablespoons sweet chilli sauce, then toss to mix and serve immediately.

lamb with sugar snap peas

Serves **4**
Preparation time **10 minutes**,
  plus marinating
Cooking time **10 minutes**

2 teaspoons **cornflour**
1½ tablespoons **Shaoxing
  rice wine**
2 tablespoons **light soy sauce**
2 **garlic cloves**, finely chopped
500 g (1 lb) boneless lean
  lamb leg steaks, cut into
  thin slices
1 teaspoon **Szechuan
  peppercorns**
¼ teaspoon **rock salt**
3 tablespoons **groundnut oil**
75 g (3 oz) **sugar snap peas**,
  trimmed and sliced into thirds
1 teaspoon **sesame oil**
1 **red chilli**, deseeded and
  finely chopped
1 **spring onion**, very finely
  shredded

Mix the cornflour with the rice wine in a bowl until
smooth, then stir in the soy sauce and garlic. Add the
lamb and toss to coat evenly. Cover and leave to
marinate at room temperature for 25–30 minutes,
then drain the lamb.

Place the Szechuan peppercorns in a dry wok or large
frying pan and stir over a medium heat until they begin
to pop and release their aroma. Transfer to a mortar, add
the salt and pound with a pestle until coarsely ground.

Heat half the groundnut oil in the pan over a high heat
until the oil starts to shimmer. Add half the lamb and
stir-fry for 3 minutes, then remove with a slotted spoon.
Add the remaining groundnut oil to the pan and stir-fry
the rest of the lamb in the same way.

Return all the lamb to the pan, add the sugar snap
peas and stir-fry for 1 minute. Add the sesame oil, chilli,
spring onion and the ground salt and pepper mixture
and stir-fry for a further minute. Serve immediately with
noodles, if liked.

For scallops with mangetout & Szechuan pepper,
follow the recipe above, replacing the lamb with
12 cleaned scallops. After marinating as above, stir-fry
in 2 batches as above. Return to the pan and add 75 g
(3 oz) halved mangetout instead of the sugar snap peas
with the other ingredients, then continue as above.

beef with yellow peppers

Serves **4**

Preparation time **10 minutes**

Cooking time **8 minutes**

½ tablespoon **groundnut oil**

1 tablespoon **black bean sauce**

400 g (13 oz) **rump** or **fillet steak**, sliced

1 **red chilli**, deseeded and cut into strips

100 g (3½ oz) **onion**, cut into squares

300 g (10 oz) **yellow peppers**, cored, deseeded and cut into squares

200 ml (7 fl oz) boiling hot **beef stock**

1 teaspoon **cornflour**, mixed to a paste with 1 tablespoon **cold water**

Heat the oil in a wok or large frying pan over a high heat until the oil starts to shimmer. Add the black bean sauce and stir-fry for a few seconds, then add the sliced beef and stir-fry for about 1 minute until half-cooked.

Mix in the chilli, onion and yellow peppers and stir-fry for 1–2 minutes, then add the hot stock and bring to the boil.

Stir in the cornflour paste gradually and cook, stirring constantly, until the sauce has thickened and become transparent. Serve immediately with Spicy Tomato Dipping Sauce (see below).

For spicy tomato dipping sauce, to serve as an accompaniment, heat 100 ml (3½ fl oz) passata in a wok or large frying pan with 2 tablespoons each of Shaoxing rice wine and water, 1 tablespoon light soy sauce and 1 teaspoon chilli oil. Simmer until reduced to a thick sauce, then set aside to cool before serving.

chinese barbecue pork

Serves **4–6**
Preparation time **10 minutes**,
  plus marinating and resting
Cooking time **20 minutes**

875 g (1¾ lb) lean **pork
  tenderloin fillet**
6 tablespoons **char siu sauce**
  (Chinese barbecue sauce)
2 tablespoons **clear honey**

Cut the pork in half lengthways. Using a sharp knife, cut slits into both sides of the pork in a crisscross pattern. Place the char siu sauce in a shallow glass or ceramic dish, add the pork and turn to coat evenly. Cover and leave to marinate in the refrigerator for 1 hour, or overnight if time permits.

Place a roasting rack or wire rack over a roasting tin. Pour cold water into the tin to a depth of 2.5 cm (1 inch). Lay the pork on the rack and drizzle with half the honey. Place the tin under a preheated high grill about 10 cm (4 inches) from the heat source and cook for 10–12 minutes until browned.

Turn the pork over, drizzle with the remaining honey and cook for 8–10 minutes until just cooked through. Remove from the grill, cover with foil and leave to rest for 12–15 minutes before thinly slicing. Serve with steamed rice and steamed Asian greens.

For Chinese barbecue lamb steaks, place 8 boneless lean lamb leg steaks, about 125–150 g (4–5 oz) each, in a shallow glass or ceramic dish. Mix together 2 tablespoons light soy sauce, 1 tablespoon clear honey, 2 teaspoons each of crushed garlic and fresh root ginger and 3 tablespoons char siu sauce (Chinese barbecue sauce). Brush over the lamb to coat evenly, cover and leave to marinate in the refrigerator for 1 hour. Place on a grill rack in a single layer and cook under a preheated medium-high grill for 3–4 minutes on each side, or until cooked to your liking. Serve with a crisp green salad.

five-spice beef stir-fry

Serves **4**

Preparation time **20 minutes**,
  plus marinating

Cooking time **10 minutes**

3 lean **sirloin steaks**, about
  200 g (7 oz) each
100 g (3½ oz) **sugar snap peas**
1 **carrot**
100 g (3½ oz) **baby corn**
low-calorie cooking spray
1 **red chilli**, thinly sliced
1 small **onion**, sliced
100 g (3½ oz) **broccoli florets**
300 ml (½ pint) boiling hot
  vegetable stock
2 tablespoons **light soy sauce**
1 tablespoon **cornflour**,
  mixed to a paste with
  2 tablespoons **cold water**
salt and **white pepper**
spring onions, to garnish

Marinade

2 teaspoons **Chinese
  five-spice powder**
2 **garlic cloves**, crushed
2 teaspoons ground
  Szechuan peppercorns
1 tablespoon **dark soy sauce**
½ teaspoon **dried chilli flakes**
2 tablespoons **Shaoxing rice wine**

Slice the beef into thin strips and place in a glass or
ceramic bowl with all the ingredients for the marinade.
Toss to coat evenly, cover and leave to marinate in the
refrigerator for 3–4 hours, or overnight if time permits.

Trim the sugar snap peas, cut the carrots into thin
matchsticks and halve the baby corn lengthways.

Spray a large nonstick wok or frying pan with cooking
spray and heat over a high heat. Add the beef mixture
and stir-fry for 2–3 minutes until browned and sealed.

Add the chilli and onion to the pan and stir-fry for
1 minute, then add the remaining vegetables and
stir-fry for a further 1–2 minutes. Add the stock and
soy sauce and stir well.

Bring to the boil, add the cornflour paste and stir
to mix thoroughly. Cook, stirring constantly, for
2–3 minutes until the mixture has thickened.

Remove the pan from the heat and season to taste
with salt and white pepper. Ladle into warmed bowls
and serve with steamed rice and shredded spring onion
to garnish.

For minced pork & five-spice noodle stir-fry,

follow the recipe above, replacing the steak with
625 g (1¼ lb) lean minced pork and breaking it up
with a wooden spoon while stir-frying. To serve, cook
625 g (1¼ lb) fresh egg noodles according to the
packet instructions, divide between 4 warmed wide
bowls and top with the pork and vegetable mixture.

pork with brown rice

Serves **4**
Preparation time **15 minutes**
Cooking time **30 minutes**

200 g (7 oz) **long-grain brown rice**
1 tablespoon **sunflower oil**
400 g (13 oz) boneless lean **pork**, thinly sliced, large slices halved crossways
2 **garlic cloves**, finely chopped
300 g (10 oz) **vegetables for stir-frying**, such as strips of pepper, bean sprouts, broccoli florets, sliced leeks and carrot sticks
350 ml (12 fl oz) **pressed apple juice**
2 teaspoons **tomato purée**
1 teaspoon **Chinese five-spice powder**

Bring a saucepan of water to the boil, add the brown rice and simmer for 30 minutes, or until just tender.

Meanwhile, when the rice is nearly cooked, heat the oil in a nonstick wok or large frying pan over a high heat until the oil starts to shimmer. Add the pork and garlic and stir-fry for 3 minutes. Add the vegetables and stir-fry for 3 minutes.

Mix the apple juice with the tomato purée and Chinese five-spice powder in a small bowl, pour the mixture into the pan and cook for 1 minute.

Drain the rice, spoon it into warmed bowls and top with the pork stir-fry.

For brown rice with prawns, red onion & peppers, follow the recipe above, replacing the pork with 250 g (8 oz) raw peeled king prawns and stir-frying with the garlic for 1 minute. Add 1 red and 1 green pepper, each cored, deseeded and finely chopped, and 1 thinly sliced red onion, then continue with the recipe as above.

chilli beef with spring onion

Serves **4**

Preparation time **10 minutes**

Cooking time **15 minutes**

3 tablespoons **oyster sauce**

2 tablespoons **Shaoxing rice wine**

2 teaspoons **dried chilli flakes** or 2 **dried red chillies**, halved

100 ml (3½ fl oz) **beef stock**, cooled

1 teaspoon **clear honey**

1 tablespoon **cornflour**

low-calorie cooking spray

500 g (1 lb) lean **rump steak**, very thinly sliced

12 **spring onions**, diagonally cut into 3.5 cm (1½ inch) pieces

Mix together the oyster sauce, rice wine, chilli, stock, honey and cornflour in a small bowl until smooth.

Spray a large nonstick wok or frying pan with cooking spray and heat over a high heat until smoking hot. Add the steak and stir-fry for 3–4 minutes until browned and sealed.

Stir in the oyster sauce mixture, then add the spring onions and continue cooking, stirring frequently, for 10 minutes, or until the steak is tender.

For chicken, chilli & vegetable stir-fry, follow the recipe above, replacing the beef with 500 g (1 lb) mini chicken fillets, cut in half lengthways, and adding 1 small finely julienned carrot and 100 g (3½ oz) mangetout, thinly sliced lengthways, instead of the spring onions.

poultry

chinese claypot chicken

Serves **4**

Preparation time **15 minutes**

Cooking time **20–25 minutes**

1 tablespoon **cornflour**

½ teaspoon **sesame oil**

2 tablespoons **dark soy sauce**

6 tablespoons **Shaoxing rice wine**

625 g (1¼ lb) **skinless chicken thigh fillets**, cut into bite-sized pieces

low-calorie cooking spray

3 **garlic cloves**, thinly sliced

1 tablespoon peeled and finely grated **fresh root ginger**

100 g (3½ oz) **mangetout**, trimmed

1 **red pepper**, cored, deseeded and cut into bite-sized pieces

250 ml (8 fl oz) **chicken stock**

1 **cinnamon stick**

Mix together the cornflour, sesame oil, half the soy sauce and 1 tablespoon of the rice wine in a bowl until smooth. Add the chicken and toss to coat evenly.

Spray a large nonstick wok or frying pan with cooking spray and heat over a high heat until smoking. Add the chicken and stir-fry for 4–5 minutes until lightly browned. Transfer to a plate.

Wipe the pan clean with kitchen paper, re-spray with cooking spray and heat over a medium heat. Add the garlic and ginger and stir-fry for 30 seconds, then add the mangetout and red pepper and stir-fry for a further 3–4 minutes or until tender.

Return the chicken to the pan and stir in the stock, cinnamon stick and the remaining soy sauce and rice wine. Reduce the heat to medium and simmer, stirring occasionally, for 12–15 minutes until the chicken is cooked through and the sauce is reduced. Discard the cinnamon, then serve in warmed bowls with steamed rice.

For Chinese-style minced chicken & mushroom

braise, mix together 1 tablespoon cornflour, 1 teaspoon each of sesame oil, grated garlic and fresh root ginger and 1 tablespoon each of dark soy sauce and Shaoxing rice wine in a large bowl. Add 625 g (1¼ lb) minced chicken and combine. Spray a large nonstick wok with low-calorie cooking spray and heat over a high heat. Add the chicken mixture and stir-fry for 4–5 minutes until browned. Stir in 200 g (7 oz) each of thinly sliced chestnut mushrooms and frozen peas. Stir-fry for 3–4 minutes, then stir in 250 ml (8 fl oz) chicken stock and 2 tablespoons light soy sauce. Bring to the boil, then reduce the heat and cook for 3–4 minutes until thickened. Serve with rice.

chicken & sweet chilli parcels

Serves **4**

Preparation time **15 minutes**

Cooking time **20–25 minutes**

4 **shallots**, thinly sliced

4 **skinless chicken breast fillets**, about 150 g (5 oz) each

4 tablespoons **dark soy sauce**

2 tablespoons **kecap manis**

4 tablespoons **sweet chilli sauce**

4 tablespoons **Shaoxing rice wine**

thumb-sized piece of **fresh root ginger**, peeled and cut into fine shreds

2 **garlic cloves**, finely chopped

4 **star anise**

To garnish

shredded **spring onion**

finely diced **red chilli**

Cut 4 x 30cm (12 inch) squares of foil. Place a sliced shallot and a chicken breast in the centre of each foil square. Bring the sides of each square up around the chicken to form 'cups'.

Mix together the soy sauce, kecap manis, sweet chilli sauce and rice wine in a small bowl, then divide between the parcels. Add the ginger, garlic and star anise to each parcel and fold the edges together to seal and form parcels.

Place the parcels on a baking sheet and bake in a preheated oven, 180°C (350°F), Gas Mark 4, for 20–25 minutes, or until the chicken is cooked through, opening one of the parcels and checking that the juices run clear when the thickest part of the meat is pierced with a knife.

Serve the chicken thickly sliced, garnished with shredded spring onion and red chilli, with noodles.

For steamed cod & black bean parcels, follow the recipe above, replacing the chicken with 4 thick skinless cod fillets and using 4 tablespoons black bean sauce instead of the sweet chilli sauce. Assemble the parcels as above and bake in the oven for 12–15 minutes, or until the fish is cooked through, opening one of the parcels and checking that the flesh is opaque in the centre and just flaking.

hoisin duck pancakes

Serves **4**

Preparation time **20 minutes**

Cooking time **10 minutes**

4 boneless **duck breasts,**
about 200 g (7 oz) each,
skinned

2 teaspoons **ground white**
pepper

2 **garlic cloves,** crushed

1 teaspoon peeled and grated
fresh root ginger

½ teaspoon **Chinese**
five-spice powder

2 teaspoons **sesame oil**

low-calorie cooking spray

100 ml (3½ fl oz) **hoisin**
sauce, plus extra for dipping

2 tablespoons **sweet chilli**
sauce

8 **spring onions,** shredded

½ **cucumber,** halved,
deseeded and cut into thin
matchsticks

12 **Chinese rice pancakes**

Cut the duck breasts into thin strips and place in a bowl.

Mix together the white pepper, garlic, ginger, five-spice powder and sesame oil in a small bowl.

Spray a large nonstick wok or frying pan with cooking spray and heat over a high heat. Add the duck and spices and stir-fry for about 3–4 minutes until the duck is just cooked through but still slightly pink in the centre, then add the hoisin sauce and sweet chilli sauce and cook, stirring, for 1–2 minutes until the duck is well coated with the sauce.

Transfer the duck to a warmed dish. Arrange the spring onions and cucumber in a serving bowl.

Warm the pancakes according to the packet instructions, then serve for each person to top with some of the duck, spring onions and cucumber, roll up and eat straight away with extra hoisin sauce to dip into.

For warm Chinese duck & pak choi salad, follow the recipe above to cook the duck. Spray a nonstick wok with low-calorie cooking spray and heat over a high heat. Add 2 teaspoons each of grated fresh root ginger and garlic, 1 finely chopped and deseeded red chilli and 300 g (10 oz) roughly shredded pak choi and stir-fry for about 3–4 minutes until the pak choi has wilted. Stir in the cooked duck, toss to mix well and serve on warm plates.

chicken & cashew nut stir-fry

Serves **4**
Preparation time **15 minutes**
Cooking time **10 minutes**

1 tablespoon **groundnut oil**
1 teaspoon **Szechuan peppercorns**
4 **cloves**
1 teaspoon **fennel seeds**
1 **star anise**
2 **dried red chillies**
1 **cinnamon stick**
1 **red onion**, sliced
3 large **skinless chicken breast fillets**, about 175 g (6 oz) each, thinly sliced
1 tablespoon peeled and finely chopped **fresh root ginger**
1 tablespoon **Shaoxing rice wine**
1 teaspoon **dark soy sauce**
2 tablespoons **light soy sauce**
1 tablespoon **black rice vinegar**
2 teaspoons **soft light brown sugar**
100 g (3½ oz) **raw unsalted cashew nuts**, lightly toasted
4 tablespoons **water**
6 **spring onions**, thinly sliced

Heat the oil in a large nonstick wok or frying pan over a high heat until the oil starts to shimmer. Add the whole spices and cook for a few seconds until fragrant.

Stir in the onion, chicken and then all the remaining ingredients except the measurement water and spring onions. Stir-fry for 4–5 minutes, tossing to mix well.

Add the measurement water to the pan and stir-fry for a further 3–4 minutes, or until the chicken is cooked through, then stir in the spring onions. Serve in warmed bowls with rice or noodles.

For cashew nut & spring onion fried rice, spray a nonstick wok or large frying pan with low-calorie cooking spray and heat over a high heat. Add 2 teaspoons each of peeled and grated fresh root ginger and garlic, 1 finely chopped red chilli and 6 thinly sliced spring onions and stir-fry for 1 minute. Add 100 g (3½ oz) lightly toasted raw unsalted cashew nuts and stir-fry for 1–2 minutes, then add 500 g (1 lb) cooled freshly cooked jasmine or long-grain rice and stir-fry for 3–4 minutes until it is piping hot. Serve immediately.

sesame chicken drumsticks

Serves **4**
Preparation time **10 minutes**,
  plus marinating
Cooking time **45–50 minutes**

12 large **chicken drumsticks**,
  skinned
lettuce leaves, to serve

Marinade
2 teaspoons grated **fresh root
  ginger**
2 teaspoons grated **garlic**
2 teaspoons **Chinese
  five-spice powder**
6 tablespoons **soy sauce**
6 tablespoons **sweet chilli
  sauce**
3 tablespoons **tomato purée**
finely grated rind and juice of
  1 **orange**
1 teaspoon **sesame oil**

Make 3–4 slashes in each chicken drumstick with a sharp knife and place in a glass or ceramic bowl.

Mix together all the marinade ingredients in a small bowl and then pour over the chicken. Toss to coat evenly, cover and leave to marinate in the refrigerator for 6–8 hours, or overnight if time permits, turning the chicken occasionally.

Tip the chicken and marinade into a nonstick roasting tin and arrange the chicken in an even layer. Roast in a preheated oven, 200°C (400°F), Gas Mark 6, turning occasionally and basting with the marinade and juices, for 45–50 minutes, or until sticky and golden and cooked through – the juices should run clear when the thickest part of the meat is pierced with a knife.

Serve the chicken warm or at room temperature on a bed of lettuce leaves with steamed rice.

For stir-fry sesame beef, slice 4 lean sirloin steaks, about 200 g (7 oz) each, very thinly and place in a bowl with the marinade ingredients as above. Cover and leave to marinate in the refrigerator for 1–2 hours, or longer if time permits. Spray a large nonstick wok or frying pan with low-calorie cooking spray and heat over a high heat. Add the beef and marinade and stir-fry for about 4–5 minutes until just cooked through. Serve with rice or noodles.

stir-fried duck breast salad

Serves **4**

Preparation time **15 minutes**,
  plus cooling

Cooking time **5 minutes**

3 tablespoons **groundnut oil**

500 g (1 lb) boneless,
  skinless duck breasts, cut
  into thin slices

1 **carrot**

10 cm (4 inch) piece of
  cucumber

150 g (5 oz) **iceberg lettuce**,
  finely shredded

1 **celery stick**, thinly sliced
  diagonally

4 **spring onions**, thinly sliced
  diagonally

handful of **mint leaves**, torn

salt and **black pepper**

Dressing

3 tablespoons **light olive oil**

2 tablespoons **malt vinegar**

2 tablespoons **light soy sauce**

2 teaspoons **light muscovado**
  sugar

Heat half the oil in a nonstick wok or large frying pan over a high heat until the oil starts to shimmer. Toss in half the duck, season with salt and pepper and stir-fry for about 2 minutes until browned but still slightly pink in the centre. Remove with a slotted spoon and wipe the pan clean with kitchen paper. Heat the remaining oil in the pan and stir-fry the rest of the duck in the same way.

Toss the cooked duck in a large bowl with all the ingredients for the dressing. Leave to stand at room temperature while you prepare the rest of the salad.

Use a vegetable peeler to slice the carrot thinly lengthways into paper-thin ribbons. Cut the cucumber in half lengthways and scoop out the seeds using a spoon. Place cut-side down on a chopping board and thinly slice diagonally.

Place the carrot and cucumber in a large bowl, then add the lettuce, celery, spring onions and mint.

Leave the duck to cool completely in the dressing, then toss it with the prepared salad.

For crunchy scallop salad, heat 2 tablespoons groundnut oil in a wok or large frying pan, add 12 cleaned scallops and stir-fry for about 4 minutes until golden and just cooked. Toss in a large bowl with the dressing ingredients as above, then leave to stand while you prepare the rest of the salad following the recipe above. Once the scallops are completely cooled, toss with the prepared salad.

chicken & chestnut braise

Serves **4**
Preparation time **10 minutes**
Cooking time **50 minutes**

8 large bone-in **chicken thighs**, skinned
2 tablespoons peeled and grated **fresh root ginger**
6 **spring onions**, roughly sliced
400 g (13 oz) **cooked peeled chestnuts**
4 tablespoons **Shaoxing rice wine**
600 ml (1 pint) **chicken stock**
1½ tablespoons **soft dark brown sugar**
6 teaspoons **dark soy sauce**
salt and **pepper**

Place all the ingredients in a heavy-based flameproof casserole dish and bring to the boil.

Cover the dish, reduce the heat to low (use a heat diffuser if possible) and simmer gently for about 45 minutes until the chicken is cooked through and tender, stirring occasionally.

Season with salt and pepper, then serve with steamed rice and steamed Asian greens.

For spicy lamb & mushroom stew, follow the recipe above, replacing the chicken with 625 g (1¼ lb) boneless lean lamb leg steaks, cut into bite-sized pieces, adding 3 dried red chillies and using 400 g (13 oz) thickly sliced shiitake mushrooms instead of the chestnuts. After bringing to the boil, simmer gently, covered, for about 45 minutes, or until the lamb is tender. Serve with rice or noodles.

orange roasted chicken thighs

Serves **4**

Preparation time **5 minutes**, plus marinating

Cooking time **30–35 minutes**

12 bone-in **chicken thighs**, skinned

Marinade

finely grated rind and juice of **1 orange**

2 tablespoons **dark brown muscovado sugar**

2 teaspoons **Chinese five-spice powder**

2 tablespoons **dark soy sauce**

1 tablespoon **light soy sauce**

1 tablespoon **toasted sesame oil**

Place the chicken in a single layer in a glass or ceramic dish. Mix together all the ingredients for the marinade in a small bowl and then pour over the chicken. Toss to coat evenly, cover and leave to marinate in the refrigerator for at least 30 minutes, or overnight if time permits.

Tip the chicken and marinade into a nonstick roasting tin and arrange the chicken in an even layer. Roast in a preheated oven, 190°C (375°F), Gas Mark 5, turning the chicken twice, for 30–35 minutes, or until golden and cooked through – the juices should run clear when the thickest part of the meat is pierced with a knife.

Serve the chicken hot or cold with steamed rice and steamed vegetables.

For quick orange seared scallops, place 25 large cleaned king scallops in a glass or ceramic bowl. Mix together the ingredients for the marinade as above, pour over the scallops and toss to coat evenly. Spray a large nonstick wok or frying pan with low-calorie cooking spray and heat over a high heat. Add the scallops and marinade and stir-fry for 2–3 minutes, being careful not to overcook them. Serve with cooked noodles.

kung pao chicken

Serves **4**
Preparation time **25 minutes**,
  plus marinating
Cooking time **20 minutes**

3 large skinless **chicken
  breast fillets**, about 175 g
  (6 oz) each
4 tablespoons **white wine
  vinegar**
6 tablespoons **light soy sauce**
2 tablespoons **cornflour**
6 **dried red chillies**, broken
  into pieces and deseeded
2 teaspoons **Szechuan
  peppercorns**, lightly crushed
3 tablespoons **soft brown sugar**
3 tablespoons **tomato purée**
300 ml (½ pint) **chicken stock**
low-calorie cooking spray
8 **spring onions**, diagonally
  sliced
3 **garlic cloves** finely chopped
1 **red pepper**, deseeded and
  cut into 1 cm (½ inch) pieces
400 g (13 oz) can **sliced
  bamboo shoots**, drained
400 g (13 oz) can **water
  chestnuts**, roughly chopped
100 g (3½ oz) **baby spinach
  leaves**
salt and **pepper**

Cut the chicken into 2.5 cm (1 inch) cubes and place in a wide glass or ceramic bowl.

Mix together 2 tablespoons of the vinegar, 3 tablespoons of the soy sauce, 1 tablespoon of the cornflour, the chillies, Szechuan peppercorns and half the sugar in a small bowl. Pour over the chicken and toss to coat evenly. Cover and leave to marinate in the refrigerator for about 30 minutes.

Combine the remaining vinegar and soy sauce, tomato purée and stock with the remaining cornflour and sugar.

Spray a heavy-based nonstick frying pan with cooking spray and heat over a high heat until just smoking. Add the chicken and marinade and stir-fry for 5–6 minutes, or until browned and just cooked through. Add the spring onions, garlic, red pepper, bamboo shoots and water chestnuts and stir-fry for 3–4 minutes.

Add the stock mixture and bring to the boil, stirring constantly. Reduce the heat and cook gently, stirring, for about 5–6 minutes until the sauce has thickened. Check the seasoning and adjust if necessary.

Line a shallow serving dish with the baby spinach leaves. Spoon over the chicken mixture and serve immediately.

For Szechuan pork with mangetout & carrots, follow the recipe above, replacing the chicken with 625 g (1¼ lb) lean tenderloin pork fillet, cut into small bite-sized pieces, and using 100 g (3½ oz) trimmed mangetout and 1 small carrot, cut into matchsticks, instead of the red pepper. Cook as above, then serve over steamed rice in place of the spinach leaves.

low-fat lemon chicken

Serves **4**
Preparation time **15 minutes**,
  plus marinating
Cooking time **8 minutes**

1 **egg**, lightly beaten
2 **garlic cloves**, sliced
2 small pieces of **lemon rind**,
  plus the juice of **1 lemon**
500 g (1 lb) **skinless chicken
  breast fillets**, cut into 5 mm
  (¼ inch) slices
2 tablespoons **cornflour**
1 tablespoon **rapeseed** or
  olive oil
1 **spring onion**, diagonally
  sliced into 1.5 cm (¾ inch)
  lengths
lemon slices, to garnish

Mix together the egg, garlic and lemon rind in a shallow glass or ceramic dish. Add the chicken and toss to coat evenly, then cover and leave to marinate at room temperature for 10–15 minutes.

Remove the lemon rind and add the cornflour to the marinated chicken. Mix well to distribute the cornflour evenly between the chicken slices.

Heat the oil in a nonstick wok or large frying pan over a high heat until the oil starts to shimmer. Add the chicken slices, making sure you leave a little space between them, and fry for 2 minutes on each side.

Reduce the heat to medium and stir-fry for a further minute, or until the chicken is browned and cooked through. Increase the heat and pour in the lemon juice. Add the spring onion, garnish with lemon slices and serve immediately with steamed rice.

For warm lemon chicken & herb salad, cook the chicken as above, then toss in a bowl with ½ sliced cucumber,, a handful of coriander leaves, 6 torn basil leaves and 50 g (2 oz) wild rocket. Dress the salad lightly with ½ teaspoon sesame oil and 1 teaspoon rapeseed or olive oil.

chicken & chilli stir-fry

Serves **4**
Preparation time **20 minutes**
Cooking time **15 minutes**

625 g (1¼ lb) **skinless
  chicken thigh fillets**,
  skinned and cut into thin
  strips
3 **garlic cloves**, crushed
2 teaspoons **Chinese
  five-spice powder**
1 teaspoon **dried chilli flakes**
4 tablespoons **light soy sauce**
low-calorie cooking spray
1 **onion**, cut into wedges
300 g (10 oz) **mangetout**,
  trimmed
2 tablespoons **dark soy sauce**

To garnish
small handful of **coriander
  leaves**, chopped
chilli slivers
thinly sliced **cucumber ribbons**

Combine the chicken, garlic, five-spice powder, chilli flakes and 2 tablespoons of the light soy sauce in a bowl.

Spray a large nonstick wok or frying pan with cooking spray and heat over a high heat until just smoking. Add the onion and mangetout and stir-fry for about 3–4 minutes until lightly charred and tender. Transfer to a bowl.

Wipe the pan clean with kitchen paper, re-spray with cooking spray and heat over a high heat. Add the chicken mixture and stir-fry for 4–5 minutes, or until browned and just cooked through. Return the onion and mangetout to the pan and add the remaining light soy sauce and the dark soy sauce. Cook, stirring, for about 2–3 minutes until heated through.

Ladel into warmed bowls, garnish with the coriander leaves, chilli slivers and cucumber ribbons and serve with rice or noodles.

For chilli prawn stir-fry, follow the recipe above, replacing the chicken with 625 g (1¼ lb) raw peeled tiger prawns. Cook the prawn mixture as for the chicken mixture above until they have turn pinked and are firm, then continue with the recipe.

116

spiced duck & cabbage stir-fry

Serves **4**

Preparation time **25 minutes**, plus marinating

Cooking time **20 minutes**

3 large boneless **duck breasts**, about 200 g (7 oz) each, skinned

4 tablespoons **dark soy sauce**

2 teaspoons **Chinese five-spice powder**

1 teaspoon **Szechuan peppercorns**, crushed

2 **garlic cloves**, crushed

2 teaspoons peeled and finely grated **fresh root ginger**

low-calorie cooking spray

chopped **coriander**, to garnish

Cabbage

thumb-sized piece of **fresh root ginger**, peeled and cut into thin matchsticks

2 **red chillies**, deseeded and thinly sliced

1 head of **Chinese cabbage**, shredded

1 large **carrot**, cut into thin matchsticks

3 tablespoons **light soy sauce**

2 **shallots**, halved and thinly sliced

Slice the duck thinly and place in a wide glass or ceramic bowl with the soy sauce, five-spice powder, crushed Szechuan peppercorns, garlic and ginger. Toss to mix well, cover and leave to marinate at room temperature for 20–30 minutes.

Spray a large nonstick wok or frying pan with cooking spray and heat over a high heat. Add the duck mixture and stir-fry for 5–6 minutes until browned but still pink in the centre. Transfer to a bowl, cover and keep warm.

Wipe the pan clean with kitchen paper, re-spray with cooking spray and heat over a medium-high heat. Add the ginger and chillies and stir-fry for 2–3 minutes. Add the cabbage and carrot and stir-fry for 3–4 minutes, or until the cabbage has softened. Stir in the soy sauce and shallots and continue to stir-fry for 1–2 minutes.

Transfer the stir-fried cabbage to warmed serving plates and divide the duck strips on top of each portion. Garnish with chopped coriander and serve.

For Chinese five-spice grilled duck breasts, skin 4 duck breast fillets, about 200 g (7 oz) each, score in a crisscross pattern all over with a sharp knife and place in a wide glass or ceramic dish. Mix together 4 tablespoons dark soy sauce, 2 tablespoons clear honey, 2 teaspoons Chinese five-spice powder and 1 teaspoon each of grated fresh root ginger and garlic in a bowl. Spoon over the duck and toss to coat evenly, then cover and leave to marinate in the refrigerator for at least 1 hour. When ready to cook, place the duck in a single layer under a preheated medium grill and cook for 4–5 minutes on each side, or until cooked to your liking. Thickly slice and serve immediately with steamed pak choi and rice.

chinese chicken with peppers

Serves **4**

Preparation time **10 minutes,**
plus marinating

Cooking time **20 minutes**

5 cm (2 inch) piece of **fresh
root ginger,** peeled and
grated

2 **garlic cloves,** chopped

2 **star anise**

5 tablespoons **teriyaki
marinade**

3 boneless **chicken breast
fillets,** about 175 g (6 oz)
each, diced

low-calorie cooking spray

½ **red pepper,** cored,
deseeded and diced

½ **green pepper,** cored,
deseeded and diced

½ **yellow pepper,** cored,
deseeded and diced

2 **spring onions,** sliced

300 g (10 oz) **easy-cook
long-grain rice**

600 ml (1 pint) **chicken stock**

salt and **pepper**

Mix together the ginger, garlic, star anise and teriyaki
marinade in a glass or ceramic bowl. Add the chicken
and toss to coat evenly, then cover and leave to
marinate at room temperature for 10 minutes.

Meanwhile, spray a large nonstick wok or frying pan
with cooking spray and heat over a medium heat.
Add the peppers and stir-fry for 3 minutes.

Add the spring onions, rice and chicken to the pan,
then pour over the stock. Season to taste with salt and
pepper and simmer for 15 minutes until the rice is just
tender. Serve immediately.

For pork with green peppers & lychees, follow
the recipe above, replacing the chicken with 450 g
(14½ oz) diced lean pork. Instead of the mixed peppers,
stir-fry 1½ cored, deseeded and diced green peppers
and stir a 400 g (13 oz) can lychees, drained, into the
pan with the spring onions, rice and pork.

chicken with black bean sauce

Serves **4**
Preparation time **15 minutes**
Cooking time **15 minutes**

low-calorie cooking spray
1 **red onion**, thinly sliced
2 **red peppers**, cored,
   deseeded and thinly sliced
2 **garlic cloves**, crushed
2 **red chillies**, deseeded and
   finely chopped
4 skinless **chicken breast
   fillets**, about 150 –175 g
   (5–6 oz) each, thinly sliced
6 **spring onions**, diagonally
   sliced into 3.5 cm (1½ inch)
   pieces
2 teaspoons **cornflour**
6 tablespoons **black bean
   sauce**
2 tablespoons **Shaoxing rice
   wine**
100 ml (3½ fl oz) **chicken** or
   beef stock, cooled

Spray a large nonstick wok or frying pan with cooking spray and heat over a high heat. Add the red onion and red peppers and stir-fry for 1–2 minutes.

Add the garlic, chillies and chicken to the pan and stir-fry over a very high heat for about 5–6 minutes, or until the chicken is sealed and tender. Add the spring onions and stir-fry for a further minute.

Mix the cornflour with the black bean sauce, rice wine and stock in a small bowl until smooth. Stir into the pan and cook, stirring constantly, for about 2–3 minutes until the mixture has thickened slightly. Serve with boiled or steamed rice.

For prawns with spring onion & black bean, follow the recipe above, replacing the chicken with 625 g (1¼ lb) large raw peeled king or tiger prawns. When the dish is cooked, remove the pan from the heat and stir in a small handful of finely chopped coriander leaves.

sweet & sour chicken

Serves **4**
Preparation time **20 minutes**
Cooking time **20 minutes**

300 ml (½ pint) **pineapple juice**
2 **garlic cloves**, crushed
2 teaspoons peeled and grated **fresh root ginger**
2 tablespoons **dark soy sauce**
2 tablespoons **white wine vinegar**
2 tablespoons **clear honey**
4 tablespoons **tomato ketchup**
¼ teaspoon **dried chilli flakes**
low-calorie cooking spray
1 **onion**, thickly sliced
1 **red pepper**, deseeded and cut into small bite-sized pieces
1 **yellow pepper**, deseeded and cut into small bite-sized pieces
4 skinless **chicken breast fillets**, about 175 g (6 oz) each, cut into bite-sized pieces
200 g (7 oz) **cubed pineapple**
2 tablespoons **cornflour**, mixed to a paste with
4 tablespoons **cold water**

Place the pineapple juice in a large measuring jug and stir in the garlic, ginger, soy sauce, vinegar, honey, ketchup and chilli flakes until thoroughly combined. Set aside.

Spray a large nonstick wok or frying pan with cooking spray and heat over a high heat. Add the onion and peppers and stir-fry for about 3–4 minutes until just tender. Add the chicken and stir-fry for 4–5 minutes until very lightly browned.

Add the pineapple juice mixture and pineapple chunks to the pan and bring to a simmer over a medium heat. Cook, stirring frequently, for 4–5 minutes until the chicken is cooked through.

Stir in the cornflour paste and cook, stirring constantly, for 3–4 minutes, until the sauce has thickened. Serve with noodles or Light Egg Fried Rice (see page 224).

For classic sweet & sour pork, follow the above recipe, replacing the chicken with 625 g (1¼ lb) pork tenderloin fillets, cut into bite-sized pieces. When the dish is ready, serve with egg noodles.

sticky ginger chicken stir-fry

Serves **4**
Preparation time **10 minutes**
Cooking time **10 minutes**

400 g (13 oz) **skinless chicken mini breast fillets**, halved lengthways
thumb-sized piece of **fresh root ginger**, peeled and cut into matchsticks
3 tablespoons **sweet chilli sauce**
low-calorie cooking spray
200 g (7 oz) **mangetout**, trimmed
200 g (7 oz) **baby courgettes**, thinly sliced lengthways
150 g (5 oz) **Chinese cabbage**, thickly sliced
8 **spring onions**, thinly sliced
small handful of **coriander leaves**

Mix together the chicken, ginger and 1 tablespoon of the sweet chilli sauce in a bowl.

Spray a large nonstick wok or frying pan with cooking spray and heat over a high heat. Add the chicken and stir-fry for about 4–5 minutes until lightly browned.

Add the mangetout, courgettes and cabbage to the pan and stir-fry for 4–5 minutes, or until the chicken is cooked through and the vegetables are just tender.

Stir in the spring onions and remaining sweet chilli sauce and cook for a further few seconds until heated through. Scatter over the coriander leaves and serve with steamed rice or noodles.

For quick prawn & vegetable stir-fry, follow the recipe above, replacing the chicken with 600 g (1 ¼ lb) raw peeled and deveined tiger prawns and using a 400 g (13 oz) pack ready-prepared stir-fry vegetables of your choice instead of the mangetout, courgettes and cabbage.

roasted chicken & plum sauce

Serves **4**

Preparation time **10 minutes**, plus resting

Cooking time **1½ hours**

1 **chicken**, about 1.5 kg (3 lb)

2 tablespoons **Chinese five-spice powder**

1 tablespoon **Szechuan peppercorns**, crushed

1 tablespoon **groundnut oil**

500 g (1 lb) **plums**, halved and stones removed

200 ml (7 fl oz) **Shaoxing rice wine**

150 ml (¼ pint) **vegetable stock**

2 tablespoons **clear honey**, or to taste

salt and **pepper**

Place the chicken in a roasting tin and pat the skin dry with kitchen paper. Mix together the five-spice powder, crushed Szechuan peppercorns and oil in a small bowl. Rub over the chicken as evenly as possible and season with salt and pepper. Roast in a preheated oven, 200°C (400°F), Gas Mark 6, for 30 minutes.

Place half the plums around the chicken and pour the rice wine and stock over them. Return to the oven and roast for a further 30 minutes.

Add the remaining plums to the roasting tin and continue to roast for 20–25 minutes, or until the chicken is cooked through (cover the chicken with foil if it is browning too fast) – the juices should run clear when the thickest part of the thigh is pierced with a knife.

Transfer the chicken to a warmed srving plate and leave to rest in a warm place. Heat the plum mixture in the roasting tin on the hob over a high heat. Stir in the honey to taste and season well with salt and pepper. Serve the chicken with the plum sauce, steamed Asian greens and rice or egg noodles.

For grilled duck with plum sauce, skin 4 duck breast fillets, about 200 g (7 oz) each, score in a crisscross pattern all over with a sharp knife and place in a single layer on a nonstick baking sheet. Mix together 6 tablespoons plum sauce, 2 tablespoons light soy sauce and 1 teaspoon Chinese five-spice powder in a bowl. Spoon over the duck to coat evenly, cover and leave to marinate in the refrigerator for 1–2 hours, or overnight. Cook under a preheated medium-high grill for 4–5 minutes on each side, or until cooked to your liking.

fish & seafood

sesame swordfish parcels

Serves **4**
Preparation time **20 minutes**
Cooking time **20 minutes**

4 **swordfish** or **shark fillets**,
about 200 g (7 oz) each,
pin-boned and skinned
75 g (3 oz) **shiitake**
mushrooms, sliced
50 g (2 oz) **sugar snap peas**,
halved lengthways
1 **mild red chilli**, deseeded
and thinly sliced
2 tablespoons **sesame oil**,
plus extra for brushing
40 g (1 ½ oz) **fresh root**
ginger, peeled and grated
2 **garlic cloves**, crushed
2 tablespoons **light soy sauce**
2 tablespoons **lime juice**
2 tablespoons **sweet chilli**
sauce
4 tablespoons chopped
coriander

Cut 4 x 30 cm (12 inch) squares of nonstick baking
paper and brush the centres with sesame oil. Place a
fish fillet in the centre of each square. Mix together the
mushrooms, sugar snap peas and chilli, then divide
between the paper, piling on top of the fish. Bring the
sides of each square up around the fish to form 'cups'.

Mix together the sesame oil, ginger and garlic and
spoon over the vegetables. Fold the edges of the paper
to seal and form parcels and place on a baking tray.

Bake in a preheated oven, 190°C (375°F), Gas Mark 5,
for 20 minutes, or until the fish is cooked through (open
a parcel and check the flesh is opaque in the centre).

Meanwhile, mix together the soy sauce, lime juice,
sweet chilli sauce and coriander. Loosen the parcels
and spoon the dressing over the fish before serving.

For oriental mussel parcels, divide 1 kg (2 lb)
scrubbed and debearded live mussels, discarding any
open ones that do not close when tapped, 1 finely
chopped red chilli, 2.5 cm (1 inch) piece of finely chopped
fresh root ginger and 1 chopped garlic clove between
4 large squares of nonstick baking paper. Bring the sides
of each square up around the mussels. Mix together
125 ml (4 fl oz) coconut milk and 1 tablespoon fish
sauce, season and divide between the paper squares,
then fold over the edges of the paper to seal the parcels.
Place on a baking sheet and bake in a preheated oven,
200°C (400°F), Gas Mark 6, for 6–8 minutes until all the
mussels have opened, opening up one of the parcels to
check. Discard any that remain closed. Sprinkle with a
little chopped coriander and serve with bread.

ginger & garlic prawns

Serves **4**
Preparation time **20 minutes**,
  plus marinating
Cooking time **15 minutes**

625 g (1¼ lb) **raw tiger
  prawns**, peeled with tails
  left intact
low-calorie cooking spray
1 large **onion**, thickly sliced
225 g (7½ oz) **broccoli
  florets**, cut into thin pieces
1 large **carrot**, halved and
  thinly sliced diagonally
8 **spring onions**, diagonally
  sliced into 3 cm (1¼ inch)
  lengths
2.5 cm (1 inch) piece of **fresh
  root ginger**, peeled and very
  finely shredded
100 ml (3½ fl oz) **chicken
  stock**
1 tablespoon **oyster sauce**

Marinade
6 tablespoons **light soy sauce**
4 **garlic cloves**, crushed
2 teaspoons **Szechuan
  peppercorns**, crushed
2 tablespoons **rice vinegar**
1 tablespoon **cornflour**

Place the prawns in a glass or ceramic bowl and add all the ingredients for the marinade. Toss to coat evenly, cover and leave to marinate at room temperature for 10 minutes.

Meanwhile, spray a large nonstick wok or frying pan with cooking spray and heat over a high heat. Add the onion and stir-fry for about 3–4 minutes until softened. Add the broccoli, carrot, spring onions and ginger and stir-fry for about 3–4 minutes until just tender. Stir in the stock and cook for 2–3 minutes.

Stir the prawn mixture and oyster sauce into the pan and cook, stirring, for about 3–4 minutes until the prawns have turned pink and are firm. Serve with rice or noodles.

For Chinese-style prawn salad, place 500 g (1 lb) cooked peeled prawns in a wide salad bowl with the leaves from 2 baby gem lettuces and 400 g (13 oz) halved cherry tomatoes. Mix together 1 finely chopped red chilli, 2 tablespoons each light olive oil and sweet chilli sauce, the juice of 1 lemon and 1 teaspoon each clear honey and Chinese five-spice powder in a small bowl. Season to taste with salt and pepper, pour over the salad and toss to mix well before serving.

chilli scallops with gai lan

Serves **4**
Preparation time **10 minutes**
Cooking time **10 minutes**

400 g (13 oz) **gai lan**
(Chinese broccoli), trimmed
and sliced into 6 cm
(2½ inch) lengths
20 **scallops**, shelled and
cleaned
2 tablespoons **Chinese chilli
jam** (available from Asian
grocers)
low-calorie cooking spray
2 **garlic cloves**, finely chopped
2 teaspoons peeled and finely
chopped **fresh root ginger**
1 **onion**, thinly sliced
2 teaspoons **light soy sauce**

Place the gai lan in a bamboo steamer, then cover and steam over a wok or large saucepan of boiling water (see page 14) for 2–3 minutes until just tender. Drain and keep warm.

Meanwhile, toss the scallops with 1 tablespoon of the chilli jam in a bowl. Spray a large nonstick frying pan with cooking spray and heat over a medium-high heat. Add the scallops and stir-fry for 1 minute on each side until just cooked. Remove from the pan and cover to keep warm.

Wipe the pan clean with kitchen paper, re-spray with cooking spray and heat over a medium heat. Add the garlic, ginger and onion and stir-fry for 3–4 minutes until softened. Add the remaining chilli jam and the gai lan, tossing to coat. Remove from heat and stir in the scallops and soy sauce. Ladle into warmed bowls and serve with steamed rice or noodles.

For steamed chilli scallops, shell and clean 16 scallops, reserving the shells. Place a teaspoon of Chinese chilli jam in the base of each shell, followed by the scallop. Slice 4 spring onions thinly and scatter over the scallops. Drizzle ¼ teaspoon light soy sauce over each scallop. Place in stacking bamboo steamer baskets, cover and steam over a wok or large saucepan of boiling water (see page 14) for about 5–8 minutes, depending on their size, until firm to the touch. If you don't have stacking baskets, steam in 2–3 batches; cover and keep the cooked batches warm while cooking the remainder. To serve, arrange the scallop shells on plates and serve with steamed rice and stir-fried Asian greens.

orange-soy salmon with noodles

Serves **4**
Preparation time **5 minutes**
Cooking time **13 minutes**

low-calorie cooking spray
4 **skinless salmon fillets**,
   about 175 g (6 oz) each,
   any stray bones removed
250 g (8 oz) **dried soba**
   noodles
2 teaspoons **sesame oil**
2 tablespoons **sesame seeds**
4 tablespoons **dark soy sauce**
2 tablespoons **orange juice**
2 tablespoons **mirin** (rice wine
   seasoning)

Spray a heavy-based frying pan with cooking spray and heat over a high heat. Add the salmon and cook for about 3–4 minutes on each side until browned. Remove, wrap loosely in foil and leave to rest for 5 minutes.

Cook the noodles in a large saucepan of boiling water for about 5 minutes, or according to the packet instructions, until just tender. Drain well and toss with the sesame oil and seeds.

Meanwhile, combine the soy sauce, orange juice and mirin in a small bowl. Pour into the frying pan and bring to the boil, then reduce the heat and simmer for 1 minute.

Divide the noodles between 4 warmed bowls and serve with the salmon and sauce and steamed sugar snap peas on the side.

For salmon, orange & soy parcels, cut 4 x 30 cm (12 inch) squares of foil. Place a salmon fillet in the centre of each foil square. Bring the sides of each square up around the salmon to form 'cups' and add the soy sauce, orange juice and mirin as above, along with 2 sliced spring onions, 2 sliced garlic cloves and 2 teaspoons peeled and grated fresh root ginger. Fold the edges of the foil together to seal and form parcels, place on a baking sheet and bake in a preheated oven, 200°C (400°F), Gas Mark 6, for about 15 minutes, or until the fish is cooked through, opening one of the parcels and checking that the flesh is opaque in the centre and just flaking. Remove and leave to rest briefly, then serve with steamed rice.

chinese tea-marinated trout

Serves **4**
Preparation time **10 minutes**,
  plus infusing, cooling and
  marinating
Cooking time **15 minutes**

2 **Lapsang Souchong tea
  bags** infused in 200 ml
  (7 fl oz) **boiling hot water**
1 tablespoon peeled and
  grated **fresh root ginger**
1 **garlic clove**, crushed
4 tablespoons **kecap manis**
2 tablespoons **sweet chilli
  sauce**
1 tablespoon **clear honey**
4 **trout fillets**, about 100 g
  (3½ oz) each
1 tablespoon **sesame oil**
2 tablespoons **groundnut oil**
200 g (7 oz) **baby pak choi**,
  halved lengthways

Once the tea bags have infused for 5 minutes, discard the bags. Stir in the ginger, garlic, kecap manis, sweet chilli sauce and honey until well blended. Leave to cool.

Lay the trout fillets in a shallow glass or ceramic dish and pour over the tea mixture. Cover and leave to marinate in the refrigerator for at least 4 hours, or overnight if time permits, turning the fish occasionally.

Remove the fish, reserving the marinade, and pat dry on kitchen paper. Heat the sesame oil with 1 tablespoon of the groundnut oil in a large nonstick frying pan, add the fish, skin-side down, and cook for 2–3 minutes. Turn the fish over and cook for 3 minutes. Remove to a warmed plate and cover with foil – it will continue cooking in its own steam while you cook the pak choi.

Heat the remaining oil in the pan over a high heat, add the pak choi and stir-fry until just beginning to wilt. Pour in half the reserved marinade, bring to the boil and cook for 3–4 minutes until most of the liquid has evaporated and the pak choi is tender. Serve with the trout.

For trout & prawn fishcakes, place 400 g (13 oz) trout fillets, skinned and roughly chopped, 200 g (7 oz) chopped raw peeled tiger prawns, 1 teaspoon each finely grated garlic and fresh root ginger, 1 deseeded and finely chopped red chilli, a small handful of chopped coriander, 1 beaten egg, 1 teaspoon dark soy sauce and 100 g (3½ oz) breadcrumbs in a food processor. Season with salt and pepper and process until mixed. Divide into 12 round cakes. Arrange on a baking sheet lined with lightly greased nonstick baking paper and bake in a preheated oven, 200°C (400°F), Gas Mark 6, for 15–20 minutes until lightly browned and cooked through.

squid & vegetable stir-fry

Serves **4**
Preparation time **15 minutes**
Cooking time **10 minutes**

1 tablespoon **groundnut oil**

2 teaspoons **sesame oil**

2 **leeks**, trimmed, cleaned and
very thinly sliced

2 **celery sticks**, very thinly
sliced

1 **carrot**, cut into thin
matchsticks

1 **red pepper**, deseeded and
very thinly sliced

100 g (3½ oz) **pak choi**,
roughly chopped

400 g (13 oz) cleaned **squid**,
cut into thick rings

2 teaspoons **Chinese
five-spice powder**

4 tablespoons **light soy sauce**

2 tablespoons **Shaoxing rice
wine**

3 tablespoons **sweet chilli
sauce**

salt and **pepper**

Heat the oils in a large nonstick wok or frying pan over
a high heat. Add the leeks, celery, carrot and red pepper
and stir-fry for about 3–4 minutes until softened.

Add the pak choi, squid and five-spice powder to the
pan and stir-fry for about 2–3 minutes until the squid
is just cooked through, being careful not to overcook
otherwise it will turn rubbery.

Stir in the soy sauce, rice wine and sweet chilli sauce,
season with salt and pepper and heat through, stirring.
Serve with cooked rice or noodles.

For griddled five-spice squid, place 750 g (1½ lb)
cleaned squid on a clean work surface, make a cut
down one side of each body tube and open out. Using
a sharp knife, lightly score the inside of the flesh in
a crisscross pattern to help tenderize it, then cut into
bite-sized pieces, along with the tentacles. Mix together
the juice of 1 lime, 1 tablespoon light olive oil, 1 finely
chopped red chilli and 2 teaspoons each of grated garlic
and peeled fresh root ginger and Chinese five-spice
powder in a small bowl. Rub into the squid in a shallow
glass or ceramic dish, cover and leave to marinate at
room temperature for 10–15 minutes. Heat a nonstick
ridged griddle pan until smoking hot. Remove the squid
from the marinade, add to the pan, in batches, and cook
on each side for no more than 2 minutes, pushing the
squid down with the back of a fish slice. Serve hot.

szechuan sea bass

Serves **4**
Preparation time **20 minutes**
Cooking time **25 minutes**

low-calorie cooking spray
4 thick **sea bass fillets**, about
    200 g (7 oz) each, skinned
6 **spring onions**, diagonally
    sliced into 3 cm (1¼ inch)
    lengths
2 **red peppers**, cored,
    deseeded and thinly sliced
4 **pak choi**, thickly sliced
5–6 tablespoons **water**
4 tablespoons **light soy sauce**
salt

Sauce
3 **garlic cloves**, finely chopped
2 tablespoons peeled and finely
    chopped **fresh root ginger**
2 **red chillies**, finely chopped
6 **spring onions**, finely
    chopped
2 teaspoons **Szechuan
    peppercorns**, crushed
2 tablespoons **tomato purée**
1 tablespoon **hot chilli sauce**
1 tablespoon **light soy sauce**
3 tablespoons **rice vinegar**
100 ml (3½ fl oz) **chicken
    stock**

Spray a wok or frying pan with cooking spray and heat over a medium heat. For the sauce, add the garlic, ginger, chillies and spring onions and stir-fry for about 2–3 minutes until softened. Stir in the crushed peppercorns, tomato purée and hot chilli sauce and cook, stirring, for a few seconds. Add the soy sauce, vinegar and stock to the pan, bring to a simmer and cook for about 2–3 minutes until thickened slightly.

Make 3–4 deep diagonal slashes in the skin of the fish with a sharp knife. Arrange the fillets on a baking sheet lined with baking paper, season with salt and brush all over with the sauce. Place in a preheated oven, 200°C (400°F), Gas Mark 6, for about 15–20 minutes until the fish is cooked through.

Meanwhile, spray a separate nonstick wok or frying pan with cooking spray and heat over a medium heat. Add the spring onions and stir-fry for about 1–2 minutes until softened. Add the red peppers, pak choi and measurement water and stir-fry for 3–4 minutes until the vegetables are just tender, then stir in the soy sauce. Spoon the vegetables into the centre of 4 warmed plates. Top each with a fish fillet, then spoon over some of the sauce. Serve with Quick Stir-fry Rice (see below).

For quick stir-fry rice, to serve as an accompaniment, spray a large nonstick wok or frying pan with low-calorie cooking spray and heat over a medium-high heat. Add 1 tablespoon mild curry powder, 400 g (13 oz) frozen peas and 500 g (1 lb) cooled freshly cooked jasmine or long-grain rice. Season with salt and pepper and stir-fry for 3–4 minutes, or until piping hot. Remove from the heat, stir in 6 tablespoons chopped coriander and serve.

chinese steamed oysters

Serves **4**
Preparation time **15 minutes**
Cooking time **10 minutes**

16 large **live oysters**,
   unshucked
2 **red chillies**, deseeded and
   finely diced
1 tablespoon peeled and finely
   grated **fresh root ginger**
2 teaspoons finely grated
   garlic
1 tablespoon **Shaoxing rice
   wine**
1 tablespoon **light soy sauce**
1 tablespoon **dark soy sauce**
1 teaspoon **chilli bean sauce**
1 **spring onion**, very finely
   shredded, to garnish

Divide the oysters between 2 heatproof plates that will fit inside 2 large stacking bamboo steamer baskets. Cover and steam over a wok or large saucepan of boiling water (see page 14) for 6–7 minutes, or until the oysters have opened.

Meanwhile, for the sauce, combine all the remaining ingredients in a small bowl.

Lift the oysters from the steamer baskets and carefully remove the top shell of each oyster. Spoon a little of the sauce over each steamed oyster and serve immediately with shredded spring onion and steamed rice, if liked.

For oyster & sweetcorn soup, spray a nonstick saucepan with low-calorie cooking spray and heat over a medium heat. Add 4 thinly sliced spring onions and 1 teaspoon peeled and grated fresh root ginger and stir-fry for about 3–4 minutes until the spring onion is softened but not coloured. Add 20 freshly shucked oysters, 425 g (14 oz) can creamed sweetcorn, 1 litre (1¾ pints) chicken stock and 1 tablespoon Shaoxing rice wine and bring to the boil. Reduce the heat and simmer for 5 minutes. Mix 1 tablespoon cornflour to a paste with 3 tablespoons cold water. Add to the pan and return to the boil, stirring constantly. Drizzle over 1 lightly beaten egg and cook for 2–3 minutes until the egg has set in strands. To serve, ladle the soup into warmed bowls and garnish with chopped coriander.

scallops with lemon & ginger

Serves **3–4**
Preparation time **10 minutes**
Cooking time **10 minutes**

2 tablespoons **vegetable oil**
8 **scallops**, shelled and
   cleaned, then cut into
   thick slices
½ bunch of **spring onions**,
   thinly sliced diagonally
½ teaspoon **ground turmeric**
3 tablespoons **lemon juice**
2 tablespoons **Shaoxing rice
   wine**
2 pieces of **preserved stem
   ginger with syrup**, chopped
salt and **pepper**

Heat a wok or large frying pan until hot. Add 1 tablespoon of the oil and heat over a medium heat. Add the scallops and stir-fry for 3 minutes, then remove with a slotted spoon to a plate.

Add the remaining oil to the pan and heat over a medium heat until the oil starts to shimmer. Add the spring onions and turmeric and stir-fry for a few seconds. Add the lemon juice and rice wine and bring to the boil, then stir in the stem ginger.

Return the scallops and their juices to the pan and toss until heated through. Season with salt and pepper to taste and serve immediately with Fennel & Carrot Salad (see below).

For fennel & carrot salad, to serve as an accompaniment, use a vegetable peeler to cut 1 trimmed fennel bulb and 2 carrots into thin shavings. Toss in a bowl with a handful of coriander leaves, the juice of ½ lemon and ½ teaspoon sesame oil.

mussels with black beans

Serves **4**
Preparation time **25 minutes**
Cooking time **10 minutes**

1 kg (2 lb) **live mussels**
1 tablespoon **groundnut oil**
4 **garlic cloves**, finely chopped
1 tablespoon peeled and finely
   grated **fresh root ginger**
2 **red chillies**, deseeded and
   thinly sliced
2 tablespoons **fermented
   salted black beans**, rinsed
2 tablespoons **Shaoxing rice
   wine**
500 ml (17 fl oz) **chicken** or
   fish stock
6 **spring onions**, thickly sliced
3 tablespoons **light soy sauce**
small handful of finely chopped
   coriander leaves

Clean the mussels thoroughly in cold water, scraping off any barnacles, scrubbing the shells and pulling off any stringy beards. Discard any open mussels that do not close when tapped.

Heat a large nonstick wok or frying pan over a high heat and add the oil. Add the garlic, ginger, chillies, black beans and rice wine and stir-fry for 30 seconds.

Add the mussels, stock and spring onions to the pan and cook, stirring, for about 6–8 minutes until all the mussels have opened, discarding any that remain closed.

Season the mussels with the light soy sauce. Scatter over the coriander and serve immediately, ladled into wide warmed bowls.

For mussels & black bean noodle stir-fry, spray a large nonstick wok or frying pan with low-calorie cooking spray and place over a high heat. Add 6 sliced spring onions, 1 teaspoon each of peeled and grated fresh root ginger and garlic, 400 g (13 oz) cooked mussels and 6 tablespoons black bean sauce and cook, stirring, for 2–3 minutes. Add 400 g (13 oz) fresh egg noodles and continue to cook, tossing frequently, for about 3–4 minutes until the noodles are piping hot. Serve immediately in warmed bowls.

spiced prawns with cashew nuts

Serves **4**
Preparation time **15 minutes**
Cooking time **10–15 minutes**

500 g (1 lb) **raw tiger prawns**, peeled and butterflied
1 teaspoon **Shaoxing rice wine**
1 tablespoon **egg white**
1 tablespoon **cornflour**
1 tablespoon **groundnut oil**
6 **dried red chillies**, halved and deseeded
1 teaspoon **Szechuan peppercorns**, crushed
thumb-sized piece of **fresh root ginger**, finely shredded
3 **garlic cloves**, thinly sliced
4 **spring onions**, thickly sliced
100 ml (3½ fl oz) **chicken stock**
100 g (3½ oz) **roasted cashew nuts**

Sauce
1 tablespoon **golden caster sugar**
1 tablespoon **cornflour**
2 tablespoons **dark soy sauce**
2 tablespoons **Shaoxing rice wine**
100 ml (3½ fl oz) **water**

Mix together the prawns, rice wine, egg white and cornflour in a bowl until well combined.

Stir together all the ingredients for the sauce in a small bowl until smooth and set aside.

Heat the oil in a large nonstick wok or frying pan over a high heat until almost smoking. Add the prawns and stir-fry for 3–5 minutes until just turning pink, then remove with a slotted spoon to a plate.

Add the chillies and crushed Szechuan peppercorns to the pan and stir-fry over a high heat for 1–2 minutes until fragrant. Add the ginger, garlic and spring onions and stir-fry for about 30–40 seconds.

Return the prawns with their juices to the pan and toss to mix. Add the stock and bring to the boil. Stir in the sauce mixture and cook, stirring constantly, until it has thickened. Finally, add the cashew nuts, stir to mix well and serve immediately.

For spiced prawn, mango & lemon grass rice, heat 1 teaspoon groundnut oil in a heavy-based saucepan, add 1 cinnamon stick and 2 of each chopped shallots, red chillies and garlic cloves and stir-fry for about 2–3 minutes until the shallots are softened. Add 1 tablespoon hot chilli sauce, 350 g (11½ oz) long-grain rice and 1 tablespoon lemon grass paste and stir to mix well. Pour in 600 ml (1 pint) vegetable stock and bring to the boil. Stir in 500 g (1 lb) raw peeled tiger prawns and the diced flesh of 1 mango. Cover tightly, reduce the heat to low and cook for 15–20 minutes. Remove from the heat and leave to stand, covered, for a few minutes before fluffing up with a fork and serving.

steamed ginger fish

Serves **4**
Preparation time **10 minutes**
Cooking time **6–8 minutes**

4 thick **halibut** or **cod fillets**,
    about 200 g (7 oz) each
thumb–sized piece of **fresh
    root ginger**, peeled and
    finely shredded
1 **red chilli**, deseeded and
    finely shredded
1 tablespoon finely grated
    orange rind
1 tablespoon finely grated
    lemon rind
2 **spring onions**, finely
    shredded
2 tablespoons **light soy sauce**
1 tablespoon finely chopped
    coriander leaves
salt and **white pepper**

Pat the fish dry with kitchen paper and season well salt
and white pepper. Place on a heatproof plate that will
fit inside a bamboo steamer and scatter evenly with the
ginger, chilli and orange and lemon rind.

Place the plate in the bamboo steamer, cover and
steam over a wok or large saucepan of boiling water
(see page 14) for about 6–8 minutes until the fish is
just cooked through – the flesh should be opaque in the
centre and slightly flaking but still moist.

Remove the plate from the steamer and drain off any
liquid that may have accumulated around the fish.
Scatter the spring onions over the fish, then drizzle with
the soy sauce and sprinkle over the chopped coriander.
Serve with Stir-Fry Vegetable Rice (see below) or
steamed rice and steamed Asian greens.

For stir-fry vegetable rice, to serve as an
accompaniment, spray a large nonstick wok or frying
pan with low-calorie cooking spray and place over a
high heat until almost smoking. Add 500 g (1 lb) cooled
freshly cooked jasmine rice and stir-fry for 3 minutes.
Add a 400 g (13 oz) pack mixed prepared stir-fry
vegetables and stir-fry for 5 minutes. Season well
with salt and pepper, then stir in 2 tablespoons light
soy sauce and 4 thinly sliced spring onions and cook,
stirring, for 2 minutes. Serve immediately.

salmon with asian greens

Serves **4**
Preparation time **15 minutes**
Cooking time **25 minutes**

vegetable oil, for oiling
450 ml (¾ pint) boiling hot
    water
4 chunky **salmon steaks**,
    about 200 g (7 oz) each
1 tablespoon **tamarind paste**
    blended with 175 ml (6 fl oz)
    cold water
2–3 tablespoons **light soy**
    sauce
15 g (½ oz) **fresh root ginger**,
    peeled and grated
2 teaspoons **caster sugar**
2 **garlic cloves**, crushed
1 **mild green chilli**, thinly sliced
1 teaspoon **cornflour**, mixed
    to a paste with 1 tablespoon
    cold water
250 g (8 oz) **pak choi**
8 **spring onions**, halved
    lengthways
15 g (½ oz) **coriander leaves**,
    chopped

Oil a roasting rack or wire rack and place over a roasting tin. Pour the measurement hot water into the tin. Lay the salmon steaks on the rack, cover tightly with foil and cook in a preheated oven, 180°C (350°F), Gas Mark 4, for 15 minutes, or until the salmon is almost cooked through.

Meanwhile, place the tamarind paste and water in a small saucepan. Stir in the soy sauce, ginger, sugar, garlic and chilli and heat through gently for 5 minutes.

Add the cornflour paste to the tamarind mixture and heat gently, stirring constantly, for about 1–2 minutes until thickened.

Quarter the pak choi lengthways into wedges and arrange the pieces around the salmon on the rack with the spring onions. Re-cover and return to the oven for a further 8–10 minutes, or until the vegetables have wilted.

Stir the coriander into the sauce. Transfer the fish and greens to warmed plates, pour over the sauce and serve.

For salmon with chilli & ginger bok choi, follow the recipe above to cook the salmon. Meanwhile, heat 2 tablespoons sesame oil in a wok or large frying pan over a high heat, add 1 deseeded and finely chopped red chilli, 1 cm (½ inch) piece of fresh root ginger, peeled and finely chopped, and the leaves of 3 heads of bok choi and stir-fry for 1 minute, or until the leaves have wilted. Stir in 2 tablespoons light soy sauce and serve with the cooked salmon.

sweet & sour prawns

Serves **4**
Preparation time **20 minutes**
Cooking time **10 minutes**

8 **spring onions**
3 tablespoons **sweet chilli sauce**
3 tablespoons **tomato ketchup**
1 tablespoon **soft light brown sugar**
4 tablespoons **light soy sauce**
1 tablespoon **Shaoxing rice wine**
3 tablespoons **water**
low-calorie cooking spray
thumb-sized piece of **fresh root ginger**, peeled and cut into fine matchsticks
625 g (1¼ lb) **raw king prawns**, peeled and deveined
2 **garlic cloves**, crushed
2 **red chillies**, deseeded and finely chopped
10–12 **cherry tomatoes**, halved
1 tablespoon **cornflour**, mixed to a paste with 2 tablespoons **cold water**

Cut the green tops from the spring onions and slice them lengthways into thin shreds. Set aside for a garnish. Thinly slice the white parts of the spring onions diagonally.

Mix together the chilli sauce, ketchup, sugar, soy sauce, rice wine and measurement water in a small bowl.

Spray a large nonstick wok or frying pan with cooking spray and heat over a high heat. Add the ginger and stir-fry for 30 seconds, then add the prawns and stir-fry for 2–3 minutes or until the prawns have turned pink. Remove the prawns and ginger from the pan to a plate.

Wipe the pan clean with kitchen paper, re-spray with cooking spray and heat over a high heat. Add the garlic and chillies, and as soon as they start to sizzle, add the white spring onion and cherry tomatoes and stir-fry for 30 seconds. Add the chilli sauce mixture and cornflour paste to the pan and simmer, stirring constantly, for a few seconds until thickened. Return the prawns with their juices and ginger to the pan with the shredded green spring onion and toss to mix well. Serve in warmed bowls with egg-fried rice.

For Chinese-style pan-fried prawns, spray a large frying pan with low-calorie cooking spray and heat over a high heat. Add 25 raw large king or tiger prawns, peeled and deveined, and stir-fry for 3–4 minutes until they have turned pink. Remove to a warmed serving plate. Season and scatter over 1 finely chopped red chilli and a large handful of chopped coriander. Mix together 4 tablespoons sweet chilli sauce , 2 tablespoons light soy sauce and 2 teaspoons sesame oil in a small bowl. Drizzle over the prawns, toss to mix and serve.

seafood congee

Serves **4**
Preparation time **15 minutes**,
plus soaking
Cooking time **15 minutes**

4 **dried shiitake mushrooms**
300 ml (½ pint) **boiling hot
water**
1 tablespoon **groundnut oil**
1 teaspoon peeled and grated
fresh root ginger
2 **shallots**, finely chopped
8 **live mussels**, scrubbed and
debearded
200 g (7 oz) cleaned **squid**,
cut into rings
8 **raw king prawns**, peeled
and deveined
350 g (11½ oz) freshly cooked
jasmine rice, cooled
750 ml (1¼ pints) **vegetable**
or **chicken stock**
1 tablespoon **Shaoxing rice
wine**
2 tablespoons **light soy sauce**
1 head of **pak choi**, roughly
chopped
small handful of chopped
coriander (leaves and stalks)
salt and **white pepper**

Place the dried mushrooms in a small heatproof bowl, pour over the measurement water to cover and leave to soak for 30 minutes until softened. Drain and reserve the soaking liquid. Remove and discard the stems, and dice the caps.

Heat a nonstick wok or frying pan over a high heat, add the oil and heat until almost smoking. Add the ginger, shallots and diced mushrooms and stir-fry for a few seconds.

Add all the seafood and stir-fry for about 2–3 minutes until the prawns are just beginning to turn pink. Add the cooked rice, reserved mushroom soaking liquid and stock and bring to the boil.

Stir in the rice wine and soy sauce and season to taste with salt and white pepper. Add the pak choi and coriander and gently simmer for 6–8 minutes until the seafood is cooked through and all the mussels have opened, discarding any that remain closed. Serve immediately, ladled into warmed bowls.

For spicy seafood omelette, to serve 2, beat 4 eggs in a bowl with 1 tablespoon light soy sauce, 1 teaspoon hot chilli sauce and a small handful of chopped coriander. Heat 1 tablespoon groundnut oil in a nonstick frying pan over a high heat, pour in the egg mixture and swirl to coat the base of the pan evenly. Cook for about 6–8 minutes or until almost cooked through and just set. Scatter over 6 finely chopped spring onions and 200 g (7 oz) cooked mixed seafood, fold over the sides of the omelette to enclose the filling, then flip over and serve warm with a crisp green salad.

cantonese steamed fish

Serves **4**
Preparation time **15 minutes**
Cooking time **15–18 minutes**

2 whole **sea bass**, about
   400 g (13 oz) each, cleaned
   and scaled
2 teaspoons **sea salt**
thumb-sized piece of **fresh**
   root ginger, peeled and
   finely shredded
4 **spring onions**, finely
   shredded
1 **red chilli**, deseeded and
   finely chopped
3 tablespoons **dark soy sauce**
3 tablespoons **light soy sauce**
2 teaspoons **sesame oil**
1 tablespoon **groundnut oil**

Make 3–4 deep diagonal slashes in the sides of the fish with a sharp knife. Rub the salt into the slashes and inside the cavity. Place the fish on a heatproof plate that will fit inside a steamer and scatter the ginger over the top.

Place the plate in the steamer, cover and steam for about 12–15 minutes until the fish is just cooked through – the flesh should be opaque in the centre and slightly flaking but still moist. Remove the plate from the steamer and drain off any liquid from around the fish. Transfer to a warmed shallow serving plate. Scatter the spring onions and chilli over the fish, then drizzle with the dark and light soy sauces.

Heat the oils together in a small saucepan until smoking, then drizzle over the fish. Serve with boiled rice.

For spring onion & ginger fishcakes, place 400 g (13 oz) roughly chopped raw peeled prawns, 300 g (10 oz) roughly chopped skinless cod fillet, 6 finely chopped spring onions, 1 deseeded chopped red chilli, 2 teaspoons grated fresh root ginger, 1 teaspoon grated garlic, 1 tablespoon light soy sauce and a small handful of finely chopped coriander in a food processor and process until fairly smooth. Transfer to a bowl, cover and chill in the refrigerator for 6–8 hours. Using slightly wet hands, divide the mixture into 20 portions and shape each into a round cake. Lightly spray a grill rack with low-calorie cooking spray and arrange the fishcakes on the rack in a single layer. Lightly spray the fishcakes with cooking spray and cook under a preheated medium grill for 10 minutes, turning halfway, until cooked through and golden brown. Serve with Sweet Chilli Dipping Sauce (see page 26).

fish in chilli bean sauce

Serves **4**
Preparation time **20 minutes**
Cooking time **10–15 minutes**

625 g (1¼ lb) **cod** or **halibut fillets**, skinned
3 tablespoons **cornflour**
low-calorie cooking spray
6 **spring onions**, thickly sliced diagonally
2 teaspoons finely grated **garlic**
1 tablespoon peeled and finely grated **fresh root ginger**
salt and **white pepper**

Sauce
250 ml (8 fl oz) **chicken stock**
2 teaspoons **yellow bean sauce**
1 tablespoon **chilli bean sauce**
2 tablespoons **Shaoxing rice wine**
2 teaspoons **dark soy sauce**
2 teaspoons **sesame oil**

Season the fish fillets evenly on both sides with salt. Cut the fish into bite-sized pieces and lightly dust with the cornflour to coat evenly.

Spray a nonstick wok or large frying pan with cooking spray and heat over a medium heat. Add the fish and fry for 1–2 minutes on each side until lightly browned. Remove from the pan to a plate.

Wipe the pan clean with kitchen paper, re-spray with cooking spray and heat over a high heat. Add the spring onions, garlic and ginger and stir-fry for 30 seconds.

Stir all the sauce ingredients into the pan and season to taste with salt and white pepper. Bring the mixture to the boil, then reduce the heat to a simmer and return the fish to the pan. Simmer for about 4–5 minutes until the fish is cooked through, then serve immediately with steamed rice.

For chilli bean salmon salad, arrange a 200 g (7 oz) bag of mixed salad leaves on a large salad platter. Break 500 g (1 lb) poached skinless salmon fillets into large chunks and arrange over the leaves. Mix together the juice of 2 limes, 1 finely chopped red chilli, 6 tablespoons olive oil, 1 tablespoon chilli bean sauce and 1 teaspoon each clear honey and light soy sauce in a small bowl. Season with salt and pepper and drizzle over the arranged salad. Toss to mix well before serving.

vegetables

spicy szechuan aubergines

Serves **4**
Preparation time **20 minutes**
Cooking time **20 minutes**

2 large **aubergines**, cut into
1.5 x 3.5 cm (¾ x 1½ inch)
batons
low-calorie cooking spray
1 small **onion**, thinly sliced
4 **garlic cloves**, crushed
2 teaspoons peeled and
grated **fresh root ginger**
1 **red chilli**, thinly sliced
3 tablespoons **tomato purée**
1 teaspoon **dried chilli flakes**
1 teaspoon **Szechuan
peppercorns**, crushed
½ **red pepper**, deseeded and
cut into thin strips
½ **yellow pepper**, deseeded
and cut into thin strips
250 ml (8 fl oz) **hot vegetable
stock**
3 tablespoons **light soy sauce**
1 tablespoon **rice vinegar**
1 teaspoon **clear honey**
1 tablespoon **cornflour**,
mixed to a paste with
2 tablespoons **cold water**
6 **spring onions**, thinly sliced
chopped **mint** and **coriander
leaves**, to garnish

Spray the aubergine batons lightly with cooking spray
in a large shallow dish and toss to mix well.

Heat a large nonstick frying pan over a medium heat,
add the aubergines and stir-fry for about 3–4 minutes
until lightly browned. Remove and set aside.

Wipe the pan clean with kitchen paper, re-spray with
cooking spray and heat over a medium heat. Add the onion,
garlic, ginger and chilli and stir-fry for a few seconds.
Stir in the tomato purée, chilli flakes and crushed
peppercorns, then return the aubergines to the pan
and add the peppers. Pour in the hot stock and bring to
the boil, then reduce the heat to medium and simmer
for 5–6 minutes until the aubergine is soft and tender.
Add the soy sauce, vinegar and honey, then stir in the
cornflour paste and cook, stirring constantly, for about
3–4 minutes until the sauce has thickened.

Spoon the aubergine mixture into a large serving dish
and sprinkle with the spring onions, then garnish with the
herbs and serve immediately with jasmine rice or noodles.

For quick steamed Chinese aubergines, peel and
cut 2 large aubergines into finger-thick batons. Place in
2 stacking bamboo steamer baskets, cover and steam
over a wok or saucepan of boiling water (see page 14)
for about 10–12 minutes until tender. Transfer to a warm
plate. Make a sauce by mixing together 1 tablespoon
each of dark soy sauce, rice vinegar, chilli oil and clear
honey, 1 teaspoon crushed Szechuan peppercorns,
2 tablespoons finely chopped garlic and 1 tablespoon
finely chopped spring onion. Pour the sauce over the
aubergines and lightly toss to mix well. Garnish with
coriander sprigs and serve immediately.

broccoli with garlic & chilli

Serves **4**
Preparation time **10 minutes**
Cooking time **5 minutes**

400 g (13 oz) **broccoli florets**
2 tablespoons **groundnut oil**
2 **garlic cloves**, thinly sliced
2 teaspoons peeled and
  grated **fresh root ginger**
1–2 teaspoons **dried chilli
  flakes**
salt and **pepper**

Cut the broccoli florets lengthways into thin slices.

Bring a large saucepan of lightly salted water to the boil. Add the broccoli and blanch for 1–2 minutes. Drain and set aside.

Heat the oil in a large nonstick wok or frying pan over a high heat. Swirl the oil around, add the garlic, ginger and chilli flakes and sizzle for 20–30 seconds until fragrant.

Add the broccoli to the pan and stir-fry for about 1–2 minutes until just tender. Season with salt and pepper and serve immediately with cooked rice or noodles.

For cauliflower with garlic, chilli & sesame, follow the recipe above, replacing the broccoli with 400 g (13 oz) cauliflower florets. When the dish is ready, sprinkle over 2 tablespoons toasted sesame seeds and serve immediately.

asparagus & mangetout stir-fry

Serves **4**
Preparation time **10 minutes**
Cooking time **10 minutes**

2 tablespoons **vegetable oil**
100 g (3½ oz) **fresh root
ginger**, peeled and thinly
shredded
2 large **garlic cloves**, thinly
sliced
4 **spring onions**, diagonally
sliced
250 g (8 oz) thin **asparagus
spears**, cut into 3 cm
(1¼ inch) lengths
150 g (5 oz) **mangetout**,
trimmed and halved
lengthways diagonally
150 g (5 oz) **bean sprouts**
3 tablespoons **light soy sauce**

Heat a large nonstick wok or frying pan over a high
heat until smoking, then add the oil. Add the ginger and
garlic and stir-fry for 30 seconds, then add the spring
onions and stir-fry for a further 30 seconds. Add the
asparagus and stir-fry for 3–4 minutes.

Stir the mangetout into the pan and continue stir-frying
for 2–3 minutes until all the vegetables are slightly
softened but still crunchy.

Add the bean sprouts and toss for 1–2 minutes until
beginning to wilt, then pour in the soy sauce and toss
again. Serve immediately with steamed rice and extra
soy sauce, if liked.

For stir-fried vegetable omelettes, follow the
recipe above to cook the vegetables, then keep
warm. For each omelette, beat 3 eggs in a bowl with
2 tablespoons cold water and salt and pepper. Heat
a drizzle of groundnut oil in a nonstick frying pan over
a high heat, pour in the egg mixture and swirl to coat
the base of the pan evenly. Cook until almost cooked
through and just set. Top with a quarter of the cooked
vegetables and fold in half, then remove from the pan
and keep warm while you make another 3 omelettes in
the same way, using the remaining cooked vegetables.

noodle pancakes with asparagus

Serves **4**
Preparation time **35 minutes**
Cooking time **30 minutes**

low-calorie cooking spray
2 **garlic cloves**, crushed
1 **red chilli**, deseeded and finely chopped
1 teaspoon peeled and finely grated **fresh root ginger**
200 g (7 oz) **asparagus spears**, tough ends discarded and cut into 5 cm (2 inch) lengths
1 **carrot**, cut into matchsticks
200 g (7 oz) **mangetout**, trimmed and halved lengthways diagonally
250 ml (8 fl oz) **vegetable stock**
1 tablespoon **cornflour**
4 tablespoons **dark soy sauce**
2 tablespoons **sweet chilli sauce**
50 g (2 oz) **baby spinach leaves**
300 g (10 oz) **lo-mein noodles** (dried Chinese wheat and egg noodles), cooked according to packet instructions, rinsed with cold water and drained
1 teaspoon **sesame oil**
salt and **pepper**

174

Spray a large nonstick wok with cooking spray and heat. Add the garlic, chilli and ginger and stir-fry for 1 minute. Add the asparagus, carrot, mangetout and half the stock and bring to the boil, then gently simmer for 2–3 minutes.

Mix the cornflour and remaining stock in a bowl until smooth. Add to the pan with the soy sauce and sweet chilli sauce and simmer, stirring, for 2 minutes until thickened. Add the spinach and stir until wilted. Remove from the heat.

Spray a separate large nonstick frying pan with cooking spray and heat over a high heat. Divide the cooked noodles into 4, add 2 to the pan and flatten. Reduce the heat to medium and cook for 6–7 minutes until they develop a crust on the underside. Turn over and cook for 3–4 minutes flattening as before. Remove from the pan and keep warm while you cook the remaining 2 pancakes.

Season the vegetable mixture with salt and add the sesame oil. Seve each pancake with the vegetables on top.

For asparagus & prawn noodle stir-fry, place 250 g (8 oz) dried rice noodles in a heatproof bowl, pour over boiling water to cover and leave to stand for 5 minutes, or until tender. Drain. Spray a nonstick wok with low-calorie cooking spray and heat until smoking. Add 500 g (1 lb) raw peeled tiger prawns and stir-fry for 3–4 minutes until they turn pink. Transfer to a plate. Add 1 deseeded and thinly sliced red pepper, 1 thinly sliced onion, 200 g (7 oz) asparagus tips and 1 tablespoon grated fresh root ginger to the pan and stir-fry for 2 minutes until the onion softens. Whisk 2 tablespoons each of hoisin sauce, sweet chilli sauce and rice vinegar and 1 tablespoon clear honey in a jug. Add with the noodles and prawns to the pan and toss together for 1–2 minutes until heated through.

bitter melon with black beans

Serves **4**
Preparation time **25 minutes**
Cooking time **20 minutes**

875 g (1¾ lb) **bitter melons**
1 tablespoon **groundnut oil**
4 **garlic cloves**, finely diced
2 tablespoons peeled and
  finely diced **fresh root ginger**
2 **shallots**, finely diced
6 **spring onions**, thinly sliced
2 **red chillies**, deseeded and
  thinly sliced
4 tablespoons **fermented
  black beans**, rinsed and
  roughly chopped
2 teaspoons **golden caster
  sugar**
2 tablespoons **Shaoxing rice
  wine**
200 ml (7 fl oz) boiling hot
  vegetable stock

Cut the bitter melons in half lengthways, remove the seeds with a teaspoon and discard. Thinly slice the melons.

Bring a large saucepan of water to the boil, add the melons and blanch for 2–3 minutes. Remove with a slotted spoon and drain well on kitchen paper.

Heat the oil a large nonstick wok or frying pan over a high heat. Add the garlic, ginger, shallots, spring onions, chillies and black beans and stir-fry for 1–2 minutes. Stir in the melon, sugar, rice wine and stock and bring to the boil, then reduce the heat to medium.

Cover the pan and simmer for about 8–10 minutes until the melon is tender. Serve with steamed rice.

For broccoli with black bean sauce, spray a nonstick wok or large frying pan with low-calorie cooking spray and heat over a high heat. Add 3 finely chopped garlic cloves, 400 g (13 oz) very thinly sliced broccoli florets, 1 thinly sliced onion and 200 g (7 oz) thinly sliced shiitake mushrooms and stir-fry for about 3–4 minutes until the vegetables are slightly softened. Add 4 tablespoons black bean sauce, 2 tablespoons light soy sauce and 100 ml (3½ fl oz) vegetable stock and cook, stirring, for 2–3 minutes. Sprinkle with 1 tablespoon toasted sesame seeds and serve with noodles.

szechuan potato stir-fry

Serves **4**
Preparation time **30 minutes**,
  plus standing
Cooking time **15 minutes**

500 g (1 lb) **potatoes**
1 tablespoon **groundnut oil**
6 **garlic cloves**, roughly
  chopped
1 tablespoon peeled and finely
  chopped **fresh root ginger**
2 tablespoons finely chopped
  pickled ginger
2 teaspoons **dried chilli flakes**
1 tablespoon **golden
  caster sugar**
2 tablespoons **Shaoxing
  rice wine**
2 teaspoons **chilli oil**
2 teaspoons ground
  Szechuan peppercorns
salt and **white pepper**

Peel the potatoes, then cut into very thin matchsticks and place in a large bowl with 2 teaspoons salt. Cover with cold water and leave to stand for 8–10 minutes. Drain thoroughly and pat dry with kitchen paper.

Heat the oil a large nonstick wok or frying pan over a high heat. Add the garlic, fresh ginger, pickled ginger and chilli flakes and stir-fry for about 30 seconds. Season with salt and white pepper, then add the potatoes and gently stir-fry for a minute or so until well coated with the spices and flavourings.

Add the sugar and rice wine and continue to stir-fry for about 8–10 minutes until most of the water has evaporated and the potatoes are tender. Add the chilli oil, scatter over the Szechuan pepper and serve immediately.

For Chinese-style potato salad, place 500 g (1 lb) peeled, diced and cooked potatoes in a wide salad bowl with 6 thinly sliced spring onions, 1 deseeded and thinly sliced red chilli, a small handful of finely chopped coriander leaves and 1 deseeded and finely diced red pepper. In a separate bowl, mix together 8 tablespoons light mayonnaise, 1 tablespoon each of clear honey, light soy sauce and sesame oil and 1 teaspoon Chinese five-spice powder. Stir to mix well, season with salt and pepper to taste and pour over the potatoes. Toss to mix well and serve.

mixed vegetable stir-fry

Serves **4**
Preparation time **10 minutes**
Cooking time **15 minutes**

low-calorie cooking spray
1 **onion**, sliced
2 **garlic cloves**, crushed
1 **red pepper**, cored,
  deseeded and thinly sliced
1 **yellow pepper**, cored,
  deseeded and thinly sliced
100 g (3½ oz) **broccoli florets**
200 g (7 oz) **baby corn**, halved
8 **baby courgettes**, diagonally
  sliced into 1.5 cm (¾ inch)
  lengths
100 g (3½ oz) canned **sliced
  bamboo shoots**, rinsed and
  drained
100 g (3½ oz) canned **water
  chestnuts**, rinsed, drained
  and sliced
3 tablespoons **light soy sauce**
1 tablespoon **cornflour**
6 tablespoons **vegetable stock**
thumb-sized piece of **fresh
  root ginger**, grated and juice
  squeezed out and reserved
2 tablespoons **sweet chilli
  sauce**
50 g (2 oz) canned **bean
  sprouts**, rinsed and drained

Spray a large nonstick wok or frying pan with cooking spray and heat over a medium heat. Add the onion and garlic and stir-fry for 3 minutes, then add the peppers and stir-fry for a further 3 minutes.

Add the broccoli florets, baby corn and courgettes to the pan and continue to stir-fry for 5 minutes. Add the bamboo shoots and water chestnuts and toss to mix in.

Mix together the soy sauce, cornflour, stock, ginger juice and sweet chilli sauce in a small bowl until smooth.

Make a space in the centre of the stir-fried vegetables with a wooden spoon so that the base of the pan is visible. Pour in the sauce mixture, bring to the boil and cook, stirring constantly, until it starts to thicken. Toss the vegetables to coat thoroughly with the sauce.

Transfer to a warmed serving dish, sprinkle over the bean sprouts and serve immediately.

For quick bamboo shoot & water chestnut soup, bring 1.2 litres (2 pints) vegetable stock to the boil in a saucepan. Add 4 sliced shiitake mushrooms, 200 g (7 oz) canned sliced bamboo shoots, rinsed and drained, and 200 g (7 oz) canned water chestnuts, rinsed, drained and sliced, 1 chopped tomato and 6 sliced spring onions. Return to the boil. Mix 1 tablespoon cornflour to a paste with 2 tablespoons cold water and add to the soup mixture with 2 tablespoons light soy sauce and 1 tablespoon sesame oil. Cook, stirring, for 2–3 minutes until thickened, then ladle into warmed bowls and serve.

chinese greens in garlic sauce

Serves **4**
Preparation time **10 minutes**
Cooking time **10 minutes**

low-calorie cooking spray
6 **garlic cloves**, crushed
250 ml (8 fl oz) **vegetable
    stock**
1 tablespoon **dark soy sauce**
1 teaspoon **clear honey**
2 heads of **pak choi**, thickly
    sliced lengthways
500 g (1 lb) **choi sum**, thickly
    sliced
8 **spring onions**, cut into
    3.5 cm (1½ inch) lengths
1 tablespoon **cornflour**,
    mixed to a paste with
    3 tablespoons **cold water**
small handful of chopped
    coriander leaves
1 tablespoon peeled and very
    finely julienned **fresh root
    ginger**
1 teaspoon ground **white
    pepper**

Spray a large nonstick wok or frying pan with cooking spray and heat over a medium heat. Add the garlic and stir-fry for 1–2 minutes until lightly browned.

Pour the stock, soy sauce and honey into the pan, mix well and bring to a simmer. Add the pak choi, choi sum and spring onions and cook, stirring, for 2–3 minutes until softened.

Stir the cornflour paste into the pan, mixing well, then add the coriander, ginger and white pepper and cook, stirring constantly, for 3–4 minutes until thickened. Serve immediately with Light Egg Fried Rice (see page 224) or steamed rice.

For Chinese-style spicy runner beans, top and tail 500 g (1 lb) stringless runner beans and cut into 2.5 cm (1 inch) lengths. Cook in a large saucepan of lightly salted boiling water for 3–4 minutes. Drain and set aside. Place 2 deseeded and chopped red chillies, 4 roughly chopped shallots, 2 roughly chopped garlic cloves, 2 teaspoons peeled and grated fresh root ginger and 4 tablespoons light soy sauce in a blender and process to a smooth paste, adding a little water if needed to loosen the mixture. Spray a nonstick wok or frying pan with low-calorie cooking spray and heat over a medium heat. Add the chilli paste and stir-fry for 2–3 minutes until fragrant. Add the drained runner beans and stir-fry for 2–3 minutes until just tender. Serve immediately with Light Egg Fried Rice (see page 224).

tofu & asparagus stir-fry

Serves **4**
Preparation time **15 minutes**
Cooking time **15 minutes**

500 g (1 lb) **asparagus tips**
4 **garlic cloves**, crushed
2 **red chillies**, deseeded and
  thinly sliced
good pinch of **sea salt**
1 tablespoon **groundnut oil**
400 g (13 oz) **firm tofu**,
  drained and cut into bite-
  sized pieces
100 g (3½ oz) **roasted
  cashew nuts**
3 tablespoons **dark soy sauce**
1 tablespoon **soft light brown
  sugar**
small handful of **coriander
  leaves**, chopped
salt

Bring a large saucepan of lightly salted water to the boil, add the asparagus and blanch for 2–3 minutes. Drain and set aside.

Place the garlic, 1 of the chillies and the sea salt in a mortar and crush with a pestle to make a paste.

Heat a nonstick wok or frying pan over a high heat. Add the oil and heat until it starts to shimmer, then add the garlic and chilli paste and the remaining sliced chilli and stir-fry for 15 seconds until lightly golden.

Add the tofu to the pan and stir-fry until golden, then add the blanched asparagus and cashew nuts and stir-fry for about 4–5 minutes until just cooked. Stir in the soy sauce and sugar and stir-fry for a further 30 seconds before stirring in the coriander. Serve immediately with lime wedges and steamed rice.

For asparagus fried rice, follow the recipe above to blanch 400 g (13 oz) asparagus tips, then drain. Spray a large nonstick wok or frying pan with low-calorie cooking spray and heat over a high heat. Add the blanched asparagus and stir-fry for 1–2 minutes. Add 500 g (1 lb) cooled freshly cooked jasmine or long-grain rice, 2 tablespoons each sweet chilli sauce and light soy sauce and 1 tablespoon hot chilli sauce. Stir-fry for about 3–4 minutes until the rice is piping hot. Serve immediately in warmed bowls.

chinese wok-fried green beans

Serves **4**

Preparation time **15 minutes**

Cooking time **15 minutes**

low-calorie cooking spray

2 **garlic cloves**, thinly sliced

1 **red chilli**, deseeded and
thinly sliced

thumb-sized piece of **fresh
root ginger**, peeled and
finely shredded

6 **spring onions**, thinly sliced

6 canned **water chestnuts**,
rinsed, drained and thinly
sliced

300 g (10 oz) **green beans**

1 tablespoon **Shaoxing rice
wine**

4 tablespoons **light soy sauce**

4 tablespoons **hot water**

2 teaspoons **sesame oil**

50 g (2 oz) **roasted peanuts**,
roughly chopped

white pepper

Spray a large nonstick wok or frying pan with cooking spray and heat over a high heat. Add the garlic and chilli and stir-fry for a few seconds. Add the ginger, the spring onions and water chestnuts and stir-fry for 30 seconds.

Add the green beans to the pan and stir-fry for 5–6 minutes until they begin to blister and turn slightly brown. Add the rice wine and soy sauce and cook for a further 20–30 seconds.

Pour in the measurement water and leave the vegetables to steam for 4–5 minutes until the water has almost evaporated and the beans are cooked through but still crunchy. Stir in the sesame oil, then serve immediately scattered with the roasted peanuts.

For stir-fry mangetout with sesame & garlic, spray a nonstick wok or large frying pan with cooking spray and heat over a high heat Add 500 g (1 lb) mangetout, trimmed, and stir-fry for 2–3 minutes. Add 3 finely diced garlic cloves and stir-fry for 1 minute. Stir in 1 teaspoon caster sugar and stir-fry for 10 seconds. Pour in 100 ml (3½ fl oz) vegetable stock and simmer for 2 minutes, or until the mangetout is just tender. Stir in 1 teaspoon sesame oil and serve.

egg foo yong

Serves **4**
Preparation time **30 minutes**
Cooking time **45–55 minutes**

low-calorie cooking spray
8 **spring onions**, finely chopped
2 **garlic cloves**, crushed
1 teaspoon peeled and grated
   fresh root ginger
200 g (7 oz) **cabbage**, shredded
200 g (7 oz) canned **water
   chestnuts**, finely chopped
200 g (7 oz) **shiitake
   mushrooms**, finely chopped
1 **red pepper**, deseeded and
   finely chopped
50 g (2 oz) **bean sprouts**
8 **eggs**
1 teaspoon **dark soy sauce**
4 tablespoons **chives**, chopped
1 **red chilli**, finely chopped
salt and **pepper**

Sauce
400 ml (14 fl oz) **vegetable
   stock**
4 tablespoons **tomato purée**
3 tablespoons **dark soy sauce**
2 tablespoons **hoisin sauce**
1 tablespoon **cornflour**,
   mixed to a paste with
   2 tablespoons **cold water**

Spray a large nonstick frying pan with cooking spray and heat over a high heat. Add the spring onions, garlic, ginger, cabbage, water chestnuts, mushrooms, red pepper and bean sprouts and stir-fry for about 8–10 minutes until the vegetables are lightly browned and softened. Transfer to a large bowl and leave to cool.

Beat the eggs with the soy sauce, chives and chilli in a bowl, season with salt and pepper and then pour into the cooled vegetable mixture. Stir to mix well.

Spray a 22 cm (8½ inch) nonstick frying pan with cooking spray and heat over a medium-high heat. Add a quarter of the egg mixture, swirl to coat the base of the pan and cook for 5–6 minutes until the underside is set. Carefully flip over and cook for 3–4 minutes until cooked. Remove and keep warm. Repeat with the remaining egg mixture.

Meanwhile, for the sauce, place the stock, tomato purée, soy sauce and hoisin sauce in a small saucepan and bring to the boil. Add the cornflour paste and cook over a high heat, stirring constantly, for 3–4 minutes until thickened. Transfer each pancake to a warmed serving plate, spoon over the sauce and serve.

For cabbage, mushroom & red pepper stir-fry, spray a large nonstick wok with low-calorie cooking spray and heat. Add 2 teaspoons each of grated garlic and fresh root ginger, 4 sliced spring onions, 200 g (7 oz) each of shredded cabbage and sliced shiitake mushrooms and 2 deseeded and sliced red peppers. Stir-fry for 3–4 minutes and then add 200 g (7 oz) canned water chestnuts, drained and sliced, and 50 g (2 oz) bean sprouts. Stir in 2 tablespoons each of dark soy sauce and sweet chilli sauce and toss until mixed and heated through. Serve.

sweet chilli vegetable stir-fry

Serves **4**
Preparation time **20 minutes**
Cooking time **15 minutes**

low-calorie cooking spray

4 **garlic cloves**, very thinly
    sliced

1 teaspoon peeled and finely
    chopped **fresh root ginger**

8 **spring onions**, diagonally
    sliced

200 g (7 oz) **Chinese
    cabbage**, thinly sliced

1 **carrot**, cut into matchsticks

100 g (3½ oz) **broccoli florets**

100 g (3½ oz) **sugar snap
    peas**, trimmed

50 g (2 oz) **bean sprouts**

100 g (3½ oz) **baby corn**,
    halved lengthways

100 ml (3½ fl oz) **vegetable
    stock**

6 tablespoons **sweet chilli
    sauce**

4 tablespoons **light soy sauce**

1 teaspoon **sesame oil**

50 g (2 oz) **roasted cashew
    nuts**

2 tablespoons deseeded and
    diced **red chilli**

Spray a large nonstick wok or frying pan with cooking spray and heat over a high heat. Add the garlic, ginger, spring onions and cabbage and stir-fry for 1–2 minutes.

Add the carrot, broccoli, sugar snap peas, bean sprouts and baby corn to the pan and continue to stir-fry for 4–5 minutes until the vegetables are slightly softened.

Stir in the stock, bring to the boil and cook for 3–4 minutes.

Mix together the sweet chilli sauce, soy sauce and sesame oil in a small bowl and pour over the vegetables. Cook, stirring, for 1–2 minutes.

Scatter over the cashew nuts and chilli and serve with steamed rice or egg noodles.

For quick vegetable, noodle & sweet chilli stir-fry,
spray a nonstick wok or frying pan with cooking spray and heat over a high heat. Add a 400 g (13 oz) pack prepared stir-fry vegetables and stir-fry for 3–4 minutes. Stir in 400 g (13 oz) fresh egg noodles and 6 tablespoons each of sweet chilli sauce and water. Cook, stirring, for 2–3 minutes until the noodles are piping hot. Serve immediately.

buddha's delight

Serves **4**

Preparation time **20 minutes**,
  plus marinating

Cooking time **15 minutes**

4 tablespoons **light soy sauce**

1 teaspoon **sesame oil**

1 tablespoon **rice vinegar**

2 teaspoons **clear honey**

400 g (13 oz) **firm tofu**,
  drained and cut into 2.5 cm
  (1 inch) cubes

300 g (10 oz) **broccoli florets**

2 **carrots**, halved lengthways
  and thinly sliced diagonally

low-calorie cooking spray

1 **onion**, halved and thinly sliced

8 **spring onions**, diagonally
  sliced into 3 cm (1¼ inch)
  lengths

1 tablespoon peeled and
  grated **fresh root ginger**

2 **garlic cloves**, crushed

200 g (7 oz) **mangetout**,
  trimmed

200 g (7 oz) **baby corn**, thinly
  sliced

200 g (7 oz) canned **water
  chestnuts**, rinsed and drained

1 tablespoon **cornflour**

250 ml (8 fl oz) **vegetable
  stock**

Mix together the soy sauce, sesame oil, rice vinegar and honey in a glass or ceramic bowl, add the tofu and toss to coat. Cover and leave to marinate in the refrigerator for 1 hour. Drain the tofu, reserving the marinade.

Meanwhile, bring a large saucepan of water to the boil, add the broccoli florets and carrots and blanch for 2 minutes. Drain and then plunge the vegetables into a bowl of iced water. Drain again and set aside.

Spray a nonstick wok or large frying pan with cooking spray and heat over a medium-high heat. Add the marinated tofu and stir-fry for 5 minutes until lightly browned. Add the onion, spring onions, ginger and garlic and stir-fry for 30 seconds. Stir the blanched broccoli and carrot into the pan along with the mangetout, baby corn and water chestnuts and stir-fry for 1–2 minutes.

Mix together the cornflour, stock and reserved marinade in a small bowl until smooth and add to the pan. Bring to the boil and cook, stirring constantly, for about 2–3 minutes until slightly thickened. Serve with rice or noodles.

For tofu & vegetable stir-fry, spray a large nonstick wok or frying pan with cooking spray, add 1 tablespoon sesame oil and heat over a medium heat. Add 400 g (13 oz) firm tofu, drained and cut into 2.5 cm (1 inch) cubes, and stir-fry for about 1–2 minutes until coloured. Add 2 thinly sliced garlic cloves and stir-fry for 1 minute. Add 200 g (7 oz) each of peeled and blanched broad beans and trimmed and roughly chopped mangetout and 1 finely chopped red chilli and stir-fry for 1 minute. Spoon the vegetables on to warm plates and sprinkle over 3 tablespoons light soy sauce. Serve with steamed rice.

braised tofu with aubergine

Serves **4**
Preparation time **15 minutes**
Cooking time **15 minutes**

1 tablespoon **groundnut oil**
1 large **aubergine**, cut into
   finger-thick batons
2–3 tablespoons **water**
2 **garlic cloves**, finely chopped
1 tablespoon peeled and finely
   chopped **fresh root ginger**
1 small **red chilli**, deseeded
   and finely chopped
1 tablespoon **chilli bean paste**
200 ml (7 fl oz) boiling hot
   vegetable stock
200 g (7 oz) **firm tofu**, drained
   and cut into bite-sized squares
2 tablespooons **light soy**
   sauce
1 tablespoon **black rice**
   vinegar
2 teaspoons **soft light brown**
   sugar
6 **spring onions**, thinly sliced,
   plus extra to garnish
1 tablespoon **cornflour**,
   mixed to a paste with
   2 tablespoons **cold water**

Heat a nonstick wok or large frying pan over a high heat and add half the oil. Add the aubergine and stir-fry for about 5–6 minutes until browned and softened. Add the measurement water and cook for 1–2 minutes. Transfer the aubergine to a plate and set aside.

Add the remaining oil to the pan and heat over a high heat. Add the garlic, ginger and chilli and stir, then add the chilli bean paste and stir-fry for 30 seconds.

Pour in the hot stock, return the aubergine to the pan along with the tofu and bring to a simmer. Add the soy sauce, vinegar and sugar, then stir in the spring onions and the cornflour paste and cook, stirring constantly, for about 3–4 minutes until the mixture has thickened. Scatter with spring onions and serve with steamed rice.

For spicy braised aubergines, cut 1 large aubergine into finger-thick batons. Spray a nonstick frying pan with low-calorie cooking spray and heat over a high heat. Add the aubergine and stir-fry for 5–6 minutes until lightly browned. Remove and drain on kitchen paper. Wipe the pan clean with kitchen paper, re-spray with cooking spray and heat over a medium heat. Add 6 roughly chopped spring onions and 4 finely chopped garlic cloves and stir-fry over for about 6–7 minutes until browned. Add 1 tablespoon finely grated fresh root ginger, 2 finely chopped red chillies, 200 ml (7 fl oz) passata and 6 kaffir lime leaves and cook, stirring, for 2–3 minutes. Return the aubergine to the pan with a splash of water and simmer for 2–3 minutes. Stir in 1 tablespoon each of kecap manis, light soy sauce, clear honey, lime juice and chopped coriander. Scatter over a handful of chopped roasted peanuts and serve with rice or noodles.

pak choi with chilli & ginger

Serves **4**
Preparation time **5 minutes**
Cooking time **5 minutes**

1 tablespoon **groundnut oil**
½ **red chilli**, sliced into rings
1 tablespoon peeled and
   chopped **fresh root ginger**
large pinch of **salt**
500 g (1 lb) **pak choi**, leaves
   separated
100 ml (3½ fl oz) **water**
¼ teaspoon **sesame oil**

Heat the oil in a nonstick wok or large frying pan over a high heat until the oil starts to shimmer. Add the chilli, ginger and salt and stir-fry for 15 seconds.

Add the pak choi to the pan and stir-fry for 1 minute, then add the measurement water and continue to cook, stirring, until the pak choi is tender and the water has evaporated.

Toss in the sesame oil and serve immediately.

For pak choi & shiiitake mushrooms with chilli, ginger & oyster sauce, follow the recipe above, adding 250 g (8 oz) trimmed and sliced shiitake mushrooms with the pak choi and stirring 2 tablespoons oyster sauce into the pan with the water.

vegetable stir-fry with pak choi

Serves **4**
Preparation time **10 minutes**
Cooking time **10 minutes**

8 small **pak choi**, about
625 g (1¼ lb) in total
1 tablespoon **groundnut oil**
2 **garlic cloves**, thinly sliced
2.5 cm (1 inch) piece of **fresh
root ginger**, peeled and
finely chopped
200 g (7 oz) **sugar snap
peas**, diagonally sliced
200 g (7 oz) **asparagus tips**,
halved lengthways
200 g (7 oz) **baby corn**,
halved lengthways
125 g (4 oz) **edamame beans**
or 200 g (7 oz) **bean sprouts**
150 ml (¼ pint) **sweet teriyaki
sauce**

Cut the pak choi in half, or into thick slices if large.
Place in a bamboo steamer, cover and steam over a
wok or large saucepan of boiling water (see page 14)
for about 2–3 minutes until tender. Drain and keep warm.

Heat a large nonstick wok or frying pan over a high
heat, add the oil, garlic and ginger and stir-fry for 30
seconds. Add the sugar snap peas, asparagus tips, baby
corn and edamame beans or bean sprouts and stir-fry
for about 2–3 minutes until softened.

Pour over the sweet teriyaki sauce and toss together
until heated through. Serve immediately with the
steamed pak choi and steamed rice, if liked.

For sweet chilli vegetable stir-fry, heat a large
nonstick wok or frying pan over a high heat, add
1 tablespoon groundnut oil, 1 thinly sliced onion, 2 thinly
sliced garlic cloves and a 2.5 cm (1 inch) piece of fresh
root ginger, peeled and finely chopped, and stir-fry for
30 seconds. Add 1 carrot, cut into thin matchsticks, and
200 g (7 oz) trimmed and sliced mushrooms and stir-fry
for 2 minutes. Stir in 200 g (7 oz) bean sprouts and
300 g (10 oz) shredded spinach and stir-fry for about
1 minute until wilted. Add 200 ml (7 fl oz) sweet chilli
stir-fry sauce and toss together until heated through.
Serve immediately with the steamed pak choi as in the
recipe above or noodles.

rice &
noodles

aubergine & sesame noodle salad

Serves **4**

Preparation time **30 minutes**, plus cooling

Cooking time **30 minutes**

2 **aubergines**

1 teaspoon **chilli oil**

4 tablespoons **sesame oil**

6 tablespoons **light soy sauce**

4 tablespoons **sweet chilli sauce**

2 tablespoons **Shaoxing rice wine**

3 tablespoons **clear honey**

3 tablespoons **sesame seeds**, toasted

150 g (5 oz) **dried fine egg noodles**

1 teaspoon peeled and finely chopped **fresh root ginger**

1 **garlic clove**, crushed

25 g (1 oz) **baby spinach leaves**

1 **red pepper**, deseeded and finely chopped

8 **spring onions**, thinly sliced

50 g (2 oz) **bean sprouts**

large handful of roughly chopped **coriander leaves**

Prick each aubergine all over with a fork, place on a baking sheet and bake in a preheated oven, 200°C (400°F), Gas Mark 6, for 30 minutes, or until softened. Leave to cool.

Meanwhile, mix together the oils, soy sauce, sweet chilli sauce, rice wine and honey in a bowl. Stir in the sesame seeds and divide the dressing between 2 wide bowls.

Cook the noodles in a saucepan of boiling water for about 3 minutes, or according to the packet instructions, until just tender. Drain, add to one of the bowls of dressing and toss to coat evenly.

Mix the ginger and garlic into the remaining bowl of dressing.

Cut the aubergines in half lengthways and peel away and discard the skin. Using a spoon, scoop the flesh into the bowl of garlicky dressing. Stir in the spinach, red pepper, spring onions and bean sprouts, then add the dressed noodles and toss to mix well. Scatter with the coriander and serve.

For courgette & sesame noodle stir-fry, spray a large nonstick wok or frying pan with low-calorie cooking spray and heat over a high heat. Add 2 teaspoons each of grated fresh root ginger and garlic, 1 teaspoon sesame oil, 2 coarsely grated courgettes and 1 cored, deseeded and finely chopped red pepper and stir-fry for 2–3 minutes, then stir in 500 g (1 lb) fresh egg noodles. Add 4 tablespoons light soy sauce and 3 tablespoons sweet chilli sauce and cook, tossing, for 2–3 minutes until the noodles are just tender. Serve in warmed bowls.

beef & vegetable fried rice

Serves **4**
Preparation time **10 minutes**
Cooking time **10 minutes**

2 tablespoons **groundnut oil**
2 **garlic cloves**, crushed
2 **bird's eye chillies**, finely
chopped
2 **shallots**, cut into thin
wedges
250 g (8 oz) **lean beef**, cut
into thin strips
1 **green pepper**, deseeded
and cut into strips
125 g (4 oz) **baby corn**,
halved lengthways
125 g (4 oz) **straw
mushrooms**, trimmed
2 tablespoons **fish sauce**
½ teaspoon **demerara sugar**
1 tablespoon **light soy sauce**
300 g (10 oz) freshly cooked
jasmine rice or **long-grain
rice**, cooled
4 **spring onions**, cut into thin
rounds
handful of **coriander leaves**,
torn

Heat the oil in a nonstick wok or large frying pan over a high heat until the oil starts to shimmer. Add the garlic, chillies, shallots and beef and stir-fry for about 2–3 minutes until the beef begins to colour.

Add the green pepper, baby corn and mushrooms and stir-fry for 2 minutes.

Stir the fish sauce, sugar and soy sauce into the pan and cook for a few more seconds, then add the rice and spring onions and toss together for about 1–2 minutes until the rice is piping hot. Stir in the coriander and serve.

For mixed vegetable fried rice, follow the recipe above, omitting the beef and stir-frying the garlic, chilli and shallots for a few seconds, then stir in the remaining vegetables as above, adding 125 g (4 oz) sliced broccoli florets and 75 g (3 oz) bean sprouts. Continue with the recipe as above.

noodles with preserved cabbage

Serves **4**
Preparation time **15 minutes**
Cooking time **10 minutes**

low-calorie cooking spray
100 g (3½ oz) **Szechuan preserved cabbage**, rinsed, drained and finely chopped
4 **garlic cloves**, finely chopped
2 teaspoons peeled and finely chopped **fresh root ginger**
2 tablespoons **Shaoxing rice wine**
2 tablespoons **chilli bean sauce**
1 tablespoon **Chinese sesame paste**
1 tablespoon **dark soy sauce**
1 tablespoon **clear honey**
450 ml (¾ pint) **chicken** or **vegetable stock**
250 g (8 oz) **dried medium egg noodles**

Spray a large nonstick wok or frying pan with cooking spray and heat over a high heat. Add the preserved cabbage, garlic and ginger and stir-fry for 1–2 minutes.

Stir all the remaining ingredients except the noodles into the pan, reduce the heat to medium and simmer for 3–4 minutes.

Meanwhile, cook the noodles in a large saucepan of boiling water for about 4 minutes, or according to the packet instructions, until just tender.

Drain the noodles and divide between 4 warmed bowls. Ladle the cabbage mixture over and serve immediately.

For stir-fried rice with preserved cabbage, baby corn & bean sprouts, spray a large nonstick wok or frying pan with low-calorie cooking spray and heat over a medium-high heat. Add 2 teaspoons each grated fresh root ginger and garlic and stir-fry for 30 seconds. Add 100 g (3½ oz) Szechuan preserved cabbage, rinsed, drained and finely chopped, and 100 g (3½ oz) each sliced baby corn, trimmed mangetout and bean sprouts and stir-fry for 3–4 minutes. Stir in 500 g (1 lb) cooled freshly cooked long-grain rice, 4 tablespoons light soy sauce and 1 teaspoon chilli bean paste and toss together for about 1–2 minutes until the rice is piping hot. Serve immediately.

ants climbing a tree

Serves **4**

Preparation time **15 minutes**, plus standing

Cooking time **15 minutes**

250 g (8 oz) **dried fine bean thread noodles**

1 tablespoon **groundnut oil**

1 tablespoon peeled and finely grated **fresh root ginger**

3 **garlic cloves**, crushed

6 **shiitake mushrooms**, trimmed and thinly sliced

2 **red chillies**, deseeded and finely chopped

8 **spring onions**, finely chopped

400 g (13 oz) **minced pork**

2 tablespoons **dark soy sauce**

2 tablespoons **hoisin sauce**

250 ml (8 fl oz) boiling hot **chicken** or **vegetable stock**

1 tablespoon **cornflour**, mixed to a paste with 2 tablespoons **cold water**

200 g (7 oz) **firm tofu**, drained and cut into bite-sized cubes

Place the noodles in a large heatproof bowl, pour over boiling hot water to cover and leave to stand for 10 minutes, or until just tender. Drain and set aside.

Meanwhile, heat the oil in a large nonstick wok or frying pan over a high heat. Add the ginger, garlic, mushrooms, chillies and spring onions and stir-fry for 1–2 minutes. Add the minced pork and stir-fry, breaking it up with a wooden spoon, for about 4–5 minutes until browned.

Stir the soy sauce, hoisin sauce and stock into the pan and cook for 2 minutes. Add the cornflour paste and cook, stirring constantly, for 2–3 minutes until thickened.

Add the drained noodles and tofu and toss together for 2–3 minutes until heated through. Serve immediately.

For chicken & hoisin sauce fried rice, spray a large nonstick wok or frying pan with low-calorie cooking spray and heat over a high heat. Add 2 teaspoons each of grated fresh root ginger and garlic, 2 finely chopped red chillies and 400 g (13 oz) minced chicken and stir-fry, breaking up the chicken with a wooden spoon, for about 2–3 minutes until the chicken is lightly browned. Stir in 6 finely chopped spring onions, 500 g (1 lb) cooled freshly cooked jasmine rice and 2 tablespoons hoisin sauce and cook, stirring, for about 6–7 minutes until the rice is piping hot. Serve in warmed bowls, garnished with thinly sliced spring onions.

broccoli & mushroom fried rice

Serves **4**
Preparation time **20 minutes**
Cooking time **15 minutes**

300 g (10 oz) **tenderstem broccoli**, cut lengthways into thin slices
2 **carrots**, cut into thin matchsticks
4 large **eggs**
2 tablespoons **cold water**
low-calorie cooking spray
1 tablespoon peeled and grated **fresh root ginger**
3 **garlic cloves**, crushed
500 g (1 lb) freshly cooked **long-grain** or **jasmine rice**, cooled
200 g (7 oz) **oyster mushrooms**, trimmed
100 ml (3½ fl oz) boiling hot **vegetable stock**
2 tablespoons **light soy sauce**
1 teaspoon **sesame oil**
white pepper

Place the broccoli and carrots in a bamboo steamer, cover and steam over a wok or large saucepan of boiling water (see page 14) for about 2 minutes until tender but still crisp. Drain and set aside.

Beat the eggs with the measurement water in a bowl. Spray a large nonstick frying pan or wok with cooking spray and heat over a medium-high heat. Pour in the egg mixture and cook, stirring, for about 30 seconds until softly scrambled. Remove from pan and set aside.

Wipe the pan clean with kitchen paper, lightly re-spray with cooking spray and heat over a medium heat. Add the ginger and garlic and stir-fry for 30 seconds, then add the rice and mushrooms and stir-fry over a high heat for 3–4 minutes. Add the steamed broccoli and carrot and the stock and cook, stirring, for 3–4 minutes.

Return the scrambled egg to the pan with the soy sauce and sesame oil. Season with white pepper and stir-fry for 1 minute until the egg is heated through, then serve.

For broccoli, mushroom & carrot stir-fry, mix 1 tablespoon cornflour to a paste with 3 tablespoons cold water. Thinly slice 300 g (10 oz) broccoli florets lengthways. Cut 2 carrots into thin matchsticks and thinly slice 200 g (7 oz) shiitake mushrooms. Spray a large nonstick wok or frying pan with low-calorie cooking spray and heat over a high heat. Add the vegetables and stir-fry for 3–4 minutes. Add 5 tablespoons stir-fry sauce and 100 ml (3½ fl oz) water and cook, stirring, for 2–3 minutes. Stir in the cornflour paste and cook, stirring constantly, for about 2–3 minutes until the mixture has thickened. Serve with rice or noodles.

chicken chow mein

Serves **4**
Preparation time **20 minutes**,
  plus marinating
Cooking time **20 minutes**

4 tablespoons **light soy sauce**
1 tablespoon **hot chilli sauce**
2 teaspoons **Shaoxing rice
  wine**
4 **garlic cloves**, crushed
2 teaspoons peeled and finely
  grated **fresh root ginger**
1 teaspoon **Chinese
  five-spice powder**
3 **chicken breast fillets**, about
  175 g (6 oz) each, skinned
  and thinly sliced
200 g (7 oz) **dried fine egg
  noodles**
low-calorie cooking spray
200 g (7 oz) **sugar snap
  peas**, trimmed
200 g (7 oz) canned **water
  chestnuts**, drained and sliced
100 g (3½ oz) canned **sliced
  bamboo shoots**, drained
1 **red pepper**, deseeded and
  thinly sliced
8 **spring onions**, diagonally
  sliced into 5 cm (2 inch) lengths
4 tablespoons **sweet chilli sauce**
4 tablespoons **dark soy sauce**

Mix together the light soy sauce, hot chilli sauce, rice wine, garlic, ginger and five-spice powder in a bowl. Add the chicken and toss to coat evenly. Cover and leave to marinate at room temperature for 10 minutes.

Meanwhile, cook the noodles in a saucepan of boiling water for about 3 minutes, or according to the packet instructions, until just tender. Drain and set aside.

Spray a large nonstick wok or frying pan with cooking spray and heat over a high heat. Add the chicken mixture and stir-fry for about 4–5 minutes until lightly browned. Add all the vegetables and stir-fry for about 4–5 minutes until just tender.

Add the drained noodles to the pan with the sweet chilli sauce and dark soy sauce and toss together for 3 minutes or until the noodles are piping hot. Serve in warmed bowls.

For chicken & vegetable fried rice, spray a large nonstick wok or frying pan with low-calorie cooking spray and heat over a high heat. Add 2 teaspoons each of grated fresh root ginger and garlic and 400 g (13 oz) minced chicken and stir-fry, breaking up the chicken with a wooden spoon, for about 2–3 minutes until the chicken is lightly browned. Add 200 g (7 oz) trimmed mangetout, 200 g (7 oz) canned water chestnuts, rinsed, drained and sliced, 1 cored, deseeded and thinly sliced red pepper and 6 sliced spring onions and stir-fry for 2–3 minutes. Add 500 g (1 lb) cooled freshly cooked long-grain rice, 2 tablespoons light soy sauce and 2 teaspoons Shaoxing rice wine and toss together for about 2–3 minutes until the rice is piping hot. Serve ladled into warmed bowls.

singapore noodles

Serves **4**
Preparation time **20 minutes**
Cooking time **15 minutes**

low-calorie cooking spray
500 g (1 lb) large **raw
  tiger prawns**, peeled and
  deveined
100 g (3½ oz) lean **rindless
  bacon**, cut into small pieces
3 **garlic cloves**, crushed
1 teaspoon finely grated **fresh
  root ginger**
1 **onion**, thinly sliced
1 **carrot**, cut into matchsticks
200 g (7 oz) **sugar snap
  peas**, thinly sliced
50 g (2 oz) **bean sprouts**
1–2 tablespoons **curry
  powder** (medium or hot)
6 **spring onions**, thinly sliced
  diagonally
250 g (8 oz) **dried fine stir-
  fry rice noodles**, cooked
  according to the packet
  instructions and drained well
about 2 tablespoons **water**
6 tablespoons **dark soy sauce**
3 tablespoons **sweet chilli sauce**
2 **red chillies**, deseeded and
  thinly sliced, to garnish
salt and **pepper**

Spray a large nonstick wok or frying pan with cooking spray and heat over a high heat. Add the prawns and bacon and stir-fry for 4–5 minutes until the prawns turn pink and the bacon is golden. Remove and keep warm.

Wipe out the pan with kitchen paper. Re-spray with cooking spray and heat over a high heat. Add the garlic and ginger and stir-fry for 30 seconds. Add the onion, carrot, sugar snap peas and bean sprouts and stir-fry for 2–3 minutes until soft, then add the curry powder and spring onions and cook, stirring, for 1 minute.

Add the prepared noodles with the measurement water and toss everything together. Stir in the soy sauce and sweet chilli sauce, season with salt and pepper and stir-fry for a further minute. Return the prawns and bacon to the pan with their juices and toss through the mixture.

Divide the noodle mixture between 4 warmed shallow bowls, sprinkle with the chillies and serve with lime wedges.

For noodle & vegetable soup, divide 200 g (7 oz) cooked dried fine egg noodles between 4 warm soup bowls. Spray a nonstick wok with low-calorie cooking spray and heat until smoking. Add 1 tablespoon grated fresh root ginger and 1 thinly sliced red chilli and stir-fry for a few seconds. Add 2 tablespoons Shaoxing rice wine and 1 litre (1¾ pints) vegetable stock and bring to a simmer. Add 200 g (7 oz) thinly sliced shiitake mushrooms and 1 julienned carrot. Season with 2 tablespoons light soy sauce and 1 teaspoon each of dark soy sauce and rice vinegar. Mix 1 tablespoon cornflour with 2 tablespoons cold water, stir into the soup and cook for 2–3 minutes until slightly thickened. Stir in 50 g (2 oz) bean sprouts and 6 sliced spring onions and heat through. Ladle over the noodles and serve.

pork & prawn fried rice

Serves **4**
Preparation time **5 minutes**
Cooking time **5 minutes**

4 **eggs**
1½ teaspoons **sesame oil**
2 teaspoons **light soy sauce**
pinch of **salt**
1 tablespoon **groundnut oil**
125 g (4 oz) **raw peeled prawns**
125 g (4 oz) **cooked ham**, shredded
1 tablespoon peeled and chopped **fresh root ginger**
2 **garlic cloves**, crushed
5 **spring onions**, thinly sliced
300 g (10 oz) freshly cooked **jasmine rice**, cooled

Beat the eggs with 1 teaspoon of the sesame oil, the soy sauce and salt in a bowl until combined.

Heat ½ tablespoon of the groundnut oil in a wok or large frying pan over a high heat until the oil starts to shimmer. Pour in the egg mixture and cook, stirring constantly, for about 30 seconds until softly scrambled. Remove from the pan and set aside.

Return the pan to the heat and add the remaining groundnut oil, then add the prawns, ham, ginger and garlic and stir-fry for 1 minute until the prawns have turned pink. Add the spring onions, rice, scrambled egg and remaining sesame oil and toss together for about 1–2 minutes until the rice is piping hot.

For chicken fried rice, follow the recipe above to cook the eggs, omitting the prawns and ham. Remove from the pan, then heat 1 tablespoon groundnut oil in the pan, add the ginger and garlic as above along with 250 g (8 oz) finely chopped skinless chicken breast fillet and stir-fry for 2–3 minutes until lightly browned and cooked. Add 2 tablespoons oyster sauce and cook, stirring, for 1 minute, then tip in the spring onions and rice and continue with the recipe as above.

pork meatball noodle stir-fry

Serves **4**
Preparation time **20 minutes**
Cooking time **20–25 minutes**

500 g (1 lb) minced **pork**
2 teaspoons peeled and finely
   grated **fresh root ginger**
1 tablespoon **grated garlic**
4 **spring onions**, thinly sliced
1 **red chilli**, finely chopped
25 g (1 oz) **coriander**, finely
   chopped
25 g (1 oz) **mint leaves**, finely
   chopped
1 **egg**, beaten
1 teaspoon **salt**
1 tablespoon **kecap manis**
50 g (2 oz) **sesame seeds**
2 tablespoons **groundnut oil**
200 g (7 oz) **choi sum**, cut
   into 10–12 cm (4–5 inch)
   lengths, stalks and leaves
   separated
500 g (1 lb) **fresh egg noodles**
4 tablespoons **light soy sauce**
6 tablespoons **sweet chilli
   sauce**

To garnish
spring onion slivers
diced red chill
coriander sprigs

Place the minced pork, ginger, garlic, spring onions,
chilli, chopped herbs, egg, salt and kecap manis in a
bowl and mix well with your fingers.

Divide the mixture into 20 portions and roll each into
a ball.

Spread the sesame seeds evenly over a large plate.
Roll the meatballs in the seeds to coat.

Heat 1 tablespoon of the oil in a large nonstick wok or
frying pan over a medium heat, add the meatballs and
fry, turning frequently, for 12–15 minutes until browned
and cooked through. Transfer to a plate with a slotted
spoon and keep warm.

Wipe the pan clean with kitchen paper, add the
remaining oil and heat over a medium-high heat.
Add the choi sum stalks and stir-fry for about
1–2 minutes until just wilted. Stir in the noodles
and stir-fry for 3 minutes, or until piping hot.

Mix together the soy sauce and sweet chilli sauce
and add to the pan with the choi sum leaves and
meatballs. Toss together until heated through, then
serve immediately in warmed bowls, garnished with
spring onion, diced red chilli and coriander leaves.

For prawn & chicken meatball noodle stir-fry,
follow the recipe above, replacing the minced pork
with 250 g (8 oz) minced chicken and 250 g (8 oz)
raw peeled tiger prawns, finely chopped.

special fried rice

Serves **4**
Preparation time **30 minutes**
Cooking time **15 minutes**

low-calorie cooking spray
3 **eggs**, lightly beaten
1 tablespoon peeled and
finely diced **fresh root ginger**
4 **garlic cloves**, finely diced
1 **onion**, halved and thinly
sliced
100 g (3½ oz) **Chinese
sausage** (lap chong),
roughly chopped
100 g (3½ oz) small **cooked
peeled prawns**
1 teaspoon **golden caster
sugar**
2 tablespoons **Shaoxing rice
wine**
500 g (1 lb) freshly cooked
jasmine or **long-grain rice**,
cooled
2 tablespoons **oyster sauce**
10 **spring onions**, thinly sliced
3 tablespoons **light soy sauce**
1 teaspoon **sesame oil**

Spray a large nonstick wok or frying pan with cooking spray and heat over a high heat. Pour in the beaten eggs and swirl to coat the base of the pan evenly. Cook for about 1 minute until almost cooked through and just set. Carefully remove the omelette from the pan and drain on kitchen paper.

Roll the omelette into a cigar shape, thinly slice into thin strips and set aside.

Wipe the pan clean with kitchen paper, re-spray with cooking spray and heat over a medium heat. Add the ginger and garlic and stir-fry for 30 seconds. Add the onion and Chinese sausage and stir-fry for about 2–3 minutes until lightly browned and tender. Add the prawns and stir-fry for 30 seconds. Stir in the sugar and rice wine and cook, stirring, for 1 minute.

Add the rice, reserved omelette strips, oyster sauce, spring onions, soy sauce and sesame oil to the pan and toss together for about 3–4 minutes until the rice is piping hot. Divide the rice mixture between 4 warmed bowls and serve immediately.

For prawn fried noodles, spray a large nonstick wok or frying pan with low-calorie cooking spray and heat over a high heat. Add 2 teaspoons each of grated fresh root ginger and garlic, 6 sliced spring onions, 1 coarsely grated courgette and 1 deseeded and finely chopped red pepper and stir-fry for 2–3 minutes. Add 500 g (1 lb) fresh egg noodles, 200 g (7 oz) cooked peeled prawns, 4 tablespoons light soy sauce, 1 tablespoon sweet chilli sauce and 1 teaspoon sesame oil and toss together for about 2–3 minutes until the noodles and prawns are piping hot. Serve immediately in warmed bowls.

lamb & pak choi noodle stir-fry

Serves **4**
Preparation time **15 minutes**
Cooking time about **10 minutes**

250 g (8 oz) **dried fine egg noodles**
1 teaspoon **cornflour**
1 tablespoon **light soy sauce**
1 tablespoon **oyster sauce**
2 tablespoons **Shaoxing rice wine**
2 teaspoons **rice vinegar**
low-calorie cooking spray
300 g (10 oz) boneless lean **lamb leg steaks**, cut into thin strips
2 teaspoons peeled and finely chopped **fresh root ginger**
2 heads of **pak choi**, cut into wide strips
8 **spring onions**, thinly sliced
100 g (3½ oz) **bean sprouts**
1 teaspoon **sesame oil**
1 teaspoon **chilli oil**

Cook the noodles in a large saucepan of boiling water for about 3 minutes, or according to the packet instructions, until just tender. Drain and set aside.

Mix together the cornflour, soy sauce, oyster sauce, rice wine and vinegar in a small bowl.

Spray a large nonstick wok or frying pan with cooking spray and heat over a high heat. Add the lamb and stir-fry for about 2–3 minutes until just cooked. Remove with a slotted spoon and set aside. Add the ginger, pak choi, spring onions and bean sprouts to the pan and stir-fry for 2–3 minutes until slightly softened.

Return the lamb to the pan along with the drained noodles, sauce mixture and the sesame oil and chilli oil. Toss together for about 1–2 minutes until heated through and serve immediately.

For grilled lamb with oyster sauce and noodles,
place 8 boneless lean lamb leg steaks in a glass or ceramic dish in a single layer. Mix together 6 tablespoons oyster sauce, 2 tablespoons sweet chilli sauce and 2 teaspoons peeled and grated fresh root ginger. Spread over the steaks to coat evenly. Place the steaks on a grill rack and cook under a preheated medium-high grill for 4–5 minutes on each side, or until cooked to your liking. Serve with cooked egg noodles and Asian steamed greens.

light egg fried rice

Serves **4**

Preparation time **5 minutes**

Cooking time **5 minutes**

4 eggs

2 teaspoons peeled and chopped **fresh root ginger**

1 ½ tablespoons **light soy sauce**

2 tablespoons **groundnut oil**

300 g (10 oz) freshly cooked **jasmine rice** or **long-grain rice**, cooled

2 **spring onions**, thinly sliced

¼ teaspoon **sesame oil**

Beat the eggs with the ginger and half the soy sauce in a bowl until combined.

Heat the oil in a nonstick wok or large frying pan over a high heat until the oil starts to shimmer. Pour in the egg mixture and cook, stirring constantly, for 30 seconds or until softly scrambled.

Add the cooked rice, spring onions, sesame oil and remaining soy sauce to the pan and toss together for about 1–2 minutes until the rice is piping hot. Serve immediately.

For fried rice with Chinese leaves & chilli, follow the recipe above, adding 1 deseeded and sliced red chilli and 125 g (4 oz) shredded Chinese leaves once the rice is piping hot and tossing together for a further 30 seconds.

choi sum noodles with beef

Serves **4**
Preparation time **15 minutes**
Cooking time **10 minutes**

250 g (8 oz) **dried medium
    egg noodles**
300 g (10 oz) lean **beef
    sirloin steak**, trimmed of all
    visible fat
2 tablespoons **light soy sauce**
2 tablespoons **oyster sauce**
2 tablespoons **Shaoxing rice
    wine**
2 teaspoons **rice vinegar**
low-calorie cooking spray
1 tablespoon peeled and finely
    grated **fresh root ginger**
200 g (7 oz) **choi sum**, cut
    into wide strips
8 **spring onions**, diagonally
    sliced into 1 cm (½ inch)
    lengths
100 g (3½ oz) **bean sprouts**
1 teaspoon **sesame oil**
salt and **pepper**

Cook the noodles in a large saucepan of boiling
water for about 4 minutes, or according to the packet
instructions, until just tender. Drain and set aside.

Cut the steak into thin slices about 1 cm (½ inch) wide.
Spread out on a plate and season with salt and pepper.

Mix together the soy sauce, oyster sauce, rice wine and
vinegar in a small bowl and set aside.

Spray a large nonstick wok or frying pan with cooking
spray and heat over a high heat. Add the steak and
stir-fry for about 1–2 minutes until just cooked.
Remove with a slotted spoon and set aside. Add the
ginger, choi sum, spring onions and bean sprouts and
stir-fry for 1–2 minutes.

Return the beef to the pan along with the drained
noodles, sauce mixture and the sesame oil. Toss
together for about 1–2 minutes until heated through.
Serve in warmed bowls.

For garlic & ginger stir-fried choi sum, spray a large
nonstick wok or frying pan with low-calorie cooking
spray and heat over a high heat. Add 1 tablespoon
each of finely chopped fresh root ginger and garlic and
1 finely chopped red chilli and stir-fry for 30 seconds.
Add 500 g (1 lb) roughly chopped choi sum, 400 g
(13 oz) canned water chestnuts, rinsed, drained and
sliced, 4 tablespoons light soy sauce and 1 teaspoon
sesame oil. Stir-fry for about 1–2 minutes until the choi
sum has just wilted. Serve immediately.

tofu & shiitake egg noodles

Serves **4**
Preparation time **20 minutes**
Cooking time **15 minutes**

low-calorie cooking spray
400 g (13 oz) **firm tofu**,
    drained and cut into
    1.5 cm (¾ inch) cubes
4 tablespoons **oyster sauce**
2 tablespoons **dark soy sauce**
1 tablespoon **cornflour**,
    mixed to a paste with
    2 tablespoons **cold water**
2 tablespoons **Shaoxing rice
    wine**
200 ml (7 fl oz) **vegetable stock**
2 teaspoons grated **fresh root
    ginger**
6 **spring onions**, diagonally
    sliced into 1.5 cm (¾ inch)
    lengths, plus extra to garnish
1 **red chilli**, finely chopped
½ **red pepper**, deseeded and
    cut into thick strips
½ **yellow pepper**, deseeded
    and cut into thick strips
200 g (7 oz) **shiitake
    mushrooms**, trimmed and
    thickly sliced
400 g (13 oz) **fresh egg
    noodles**, cooked according
    to the packet instructions

Spray a large nonstick wok or frying pan with cooking spray and heat over a high heat. Add the tofu and stir-fry for about 3–4 minutes until golden. Remove and drain on kitchen paper.

Mix together the oyster sauce, soy sauce, cornflour paste, rice wine and stock in a small bowl until smooth.

Wipe the pan clean with kitchen paper, re-spray with cooking spray and heat over a high heat. Add the ginger, spring onions, chilli, peppers and mushrooms and stir-fry for 3–4 minutes. Add the sauce mixture and bring to the boil, stirring constantly. Reduce the heat, return the tofu to the pan and simmer gently, stirring occaisonaly, for 2–3 minutes.

Add the cooked noodles and toss together for about 1–2 minutes until piping hot. Serve in warmed bowls, garnished with sliced spring onion.

For shiitake & spring onion stir-fry, spray a large nonstick wok or frying pan with low-calorie cooking spray and heat over a high heat. Add 400 g (13 oz) trimmed and thickly sliced shiitake mushrooms and stir-fry for about 4–5 minutes until softened. Stir in 2 teaspoons each of finely grated fresh root ginger and garlic, 8 thickly sliced spring onions, 4 tablespoons hoisin sauce and 75ml (3 fl oz) water and bring to the boil. Mix 1 tablespoon cornflour to a paste with 3 tablespoons cold water, add to the pan and cook, stirring constantly, for about 2–3 minutes until the mixture has thickened. Remove from the heat and serve with steamed rice.

noodles with prawns & pak choi

Serves **4**

Preparation time **5 minutes**

Cooking time **15 minutes**

250 g (8 oz) **dried medium egg noodles**

3 tablespoons **vegetable oil**

2 tablespoons **sesame seeds**

2.5 cm (1 inch) piece of **fresh root ginger**, peeled and finely chopped

1 **garlic clove**, crushed

20 **raw peeled king prawns**

3 tablespoons **light soy sauce**

2 tablespoons **sweet chilli sauce**

2 heads of **pak choi**, leaves separated

4 **spring onions**, thinly sliced

2 tablespoons **sesame oil**

Cook the noodles in a large saucepan of boiling water for about 4 minutes, or according to the packet instructions, until just tender. Drain and set aside.

Add 2 tablespoons of the vegetable oil to a large nonstick frying pan and heat until almost smoking. Add the noodles so that they cover the bottom of the pan. Cook for about 3–4 minutes until golden brown and crispy on the underside. Turn over and cook on the other side until browned. Sprinkle with the sesame seeds.

Heat the remaining vegetable oil in a wok or separate large frying pan, add the ginger and garlic and stir-fry for 1 minute, then add the prawns and stir-fry for 2 minutes until beginning to turn pink. Add the soy sauce and sweet chilli sauce, bring to the boil, then reduce the heat and simmer for 1–2 minutes until the prawns have turned pink. Add the pak choi and cook, stirring, until the leaves wilt.

Place the noodles in large warmed bowls and top with the prawns and pak choi. Sprinkle with the spring onions, drizzle with the sesame oil and serve immediately.

For prawn & lemon grass stir-fry, heat 1 tablespoon vegetable oil in a large wok or frying pan over a high heat. Add 2 finely chopped shallots, 2 finely chopped lemon grass stalks, 1 deseeded and finely chopped red chilli, 1 crushed garlic clove and a 1.5 cm (¾ inch) piece of fresh root ginger, peeled and finely chopped, and stir-fry for 2 minutes. Add 20 raw peeled king prawns and stir-fry until they turn pink. Add 6 tablespoons light soy sauce, 2 tablespoons sesame oil and the juice of 1 lime and heat through, stirring. Scatter over 2 tablespoons roughly chopped coriander and serve.

tofu & vegetable fried rice

Serves **4**

Preparation time **15 minutes**

Cooking time **15 minutes**

low-calorie cooking spray

1 **red onion**, cut into thin
wedges

2 **garlic cloves**, finely chopped

1 **red chilli**, deseeded and
finely chopped

1 **carrot**, cut into thin
matchsticks

175 g (6 oz) **baby corn**,
diagonally sliced

1 bunch of **pak choi**, stems
and leaves separated

200 g (7 oz) **cherry tomatoes**,
halved

500 g (1 lb) freshly cooked
long-grain rice, cooled

2 tablespoons **sweet chilli
sauce**

2 tablespoons **light soy sauce**

200 g (7 oz) **firm tofu**, drained
and cut into bite-sized cubes

large handful of **coriander** and
mint leaves, finely chopped

Spray a large nonstick wok or frying pan with cooking
spray and heat over a high heat. Add the onion and stir-
fry for 1–2 minutes until slightly softened. Add the garlic
and chilli and stir-fry for about 1 minute until aromatic.

Add the carrot, baby corn, pak choi stems and tomatoes
to the pan and stir-fry for about 3 minutes until
softened. Transfer to a bowl.

Wipe the pan clean with kitchen paper, re-spray with
cooking spray and heat over a high heat. Add the cooked
rice and stir-fry for about 3–4 minutes until piping hot.
Add the pak choi leaves, sweet chilli sauce and soy sauce
with the reserved vegetables and toss together briefly
until heated through. Remove from the heat and stir in
the tofu and herbs. Ladle into warmed bowls and serve.

For marinated tofu with mushrooms & broccoli,

mix together 3 tablespoons each Shaoxing rice wine
and light soy sauce, 2 tablespoons sweet chilli sauce,
2 teaspoons grated fresh root ginger, 1 teaspoon grated
garlic and the juice of 1 lime in a large glass or ceramic
bowl. Add 400 g (13 oz) firm tofu, drained and cut into
2.5 cm (1 inch) cubes, and toss to coat evenly. Cover
and leave to marinate for 1 hour, turning occasionally.
Spray a large nonstick wok or large frying pan with
low-calorie cooking spray and heat over a high heat.
Add 250 g (8 oz) shiitake mushrooms, trimmed and
thinly sliced, and stir-fry for 3–4 minutes. Add 300 g
(10 oz) thinly sliced broccoli florets and continue to
stir-fry for 2–3 minutes. Add 100 ml (3½ fl oz) hot
water with the tofu and the marinade. Stir gently to mix,
cover and simmer for 4–5 minutes until the vegetables
are just tender. Serve with rice.

index

acknowledgements

Executive editor: Eleanor Maxfield
Senior editor: Sybella Stephens
Text editor: Jo Richardson
Art direction and design: Penny Stock
Photographer: William Shaw
Home economist: Sunil Vijayakar
Prop stylist: Liz Hippisley
Production controller: Sarah Kramer

Photography copyright © Octopus Publishing Group Limited/William Shaw 2014 , except the following copyright © Octopus Publishing Group/Stephen Conroy 45, 59, 133, 157, 173; Will Heap 73, 83, 91, 107, 197, 205, 217, 225; David Munns 55, 57, 231; Lis Parsons 41, 77, 121; Bill Reavell 85, 115, 149; Ian Wallace 29, 31, 139.